Someone Shot My Book

T0355745

Julie Carr

Someone Shot My Book

UNIVERSITY OF MICHIGAN PRESS

Ann Arbor

Published in the United States of America by
The University of Michigan Press
Printed and bound by CPI Group (UK) Ltd, Croydon, CR0 4YY

2021   2020   2019   2018   4   3   2   1

A CIP catalog record for this book is available from the British Library.
ISBN 978-0-472-03720-9 (paper : alk. paper)
ISBN 978-0-472-12384-1 (e-book)

For my teachers

Cover of *100 Notes on Violence*, shot through with holes. Photo credit: Laird Hunt.

Contents

Acknowledgments

Thank you to Nick Gulig for believing in my book enough to shoot it. Thanks to all the editors who have worked with me over the years on these essays: Scott Howard, Broc Rossell, Laynie Browne, David Hadbawnik, Andy Fitch, and especially Joshua Marie Wilkinson and Kazim Ali. Thank you to everyone at the University of Michigan Press, especially Susan Cronin, for excellent shepherding. Thanks to the Poetry Foundation and Jacket2 for inviting me to contribute. Thank you to the writers and friends, some of whom appear in these pages, who, through their work and love, have helped me to stay alert, to think harder, and to write better: Alexis Almeida, Aaron Angello, K. J. Holmes, Chad Kautzer, Ruth Ellen Kocher, Sara Marshall, Rusty Morrison, Fred Moten, Linda Norton, Jennifer Pap, Jeffrey Pethybridge, John-Michael Rivera, Lisa Robertson, Jeffrey Robinson, Margaret Ronda, Selah Saterstrom, Eleni Sikelianos, Oren Silverman, Sasha Steensen, Keston Sutherland, Jean Valentine, Marcus Williams, and Ronaldo Wilson. Thank you to the reading group in Denver for the slow-time. Thank you to all who have come out to Counterpath for the community and especially to HR Hegnauer for the garden. Thank you most of all to Tim Roberts for lifelong collaborations and love. This book is for my teachers, who include all named above and also Steven Goldsmith, Lyn Hejinian, Sharon Marcus, Kent Puckett, Nancy Stark Smith, and, in memoriam, Margaret Metzger, Cynthia Novack, and William Matthews. In your debt.

Some of these pieces have been published or delivered in earlier drafts in the following publications. Many thanks to editors and moderators.

"Someone Shot my Book": *The Volta Book of Poets*. Ed. Joshua Wilkinson. Portland, OR: Sidebrow Books, 2015.

"The Witch's House": *Evening Will Come: A Monthly Journal of Poetics* 4 (April 2011). http://www.thevolta.org/ewc4-jcarr-p1.html.

"By Beauty and By Fear: On Narrative Time": *Objects from a Borrowed Confession*. Boise, ID: Ahsahta Books, 2017.

"Spirit Ditties of No Tone": Originally published on *The Poetry Foundation: Harriet Blog: Craftwork* (March 2011). https://www.poetryfoundation.org. Subsequently published in *The Silence that Fills the Future* (EP Chapbook 19). Essay Press, 2015. http://www.essaypress.org/ep-19/.

"The Poet Scholar": Originally delivered as a panel paper at the session "The Poet-Scholar," moderated by Hillary Gravendyk, Modern Language Association Conference, Boston (January 2013). Subsequently published on *A. Bradstreet* (April 2013). http://www.abradstreet.com/post/46846997538/the-poet-scholar.

"I Believe That We Will Win": *Jacket2: Commentaries* (February 13, 2017). https://jacket2.org/commentary/i-believe-we-will-win.

"Another Note on Violence": *Kadar Koli: The Violence Issue*, 2012.

"In Defense of Experiences, or, The Body and the Avant-Garde": *The Force of What's Possible: Writers on Accessibility and the Avant-Garde*. Ed. Joshua Wilkinson. New York: Nightboat Books, 2014.

"No Video: On Anne Carson": *Anne Carson: Ecstatic Lyre*. Ed. Joshua Wilkinson. Ann Arbor: University of Michigan Press, 2015.

"Latin for Female Wanderer: On Lisa Robertson": Originally published on *The Poetry Foundation: Harriet Blog* (April 2012). https://www.poetryfoundation.org. Subsequently published in *Active Romanticism: The Radical Impulse in Nineteenth-Century and*

Contemporary Poetic Practice. Eds. Julie Carr and Jeffrey Robinson. Tuscaloosa: University of Alabama Press, 2015.

"On Saying No: Valentine and Dickinson *Break the Glass*": *Jean Valentine: This-World Company.* Eds. Kazim Ali and John Hoppenthaler. Ann Arbor: University of Michigan Press, 2012.

"Ralph Lemon, Fred Moten and the Unspeakable: An Improvisatory Line": Delivered as a roundtable talk at the session "Reconceiving Aesthetics Roundtable: Bodies, the Sensorium, and Contemporary Poetry," moderated by Jeanne Heuving, American Literature Association Conference, San Francisco (May 2016).

"On Property and Monstrosity": *American Poetry Review* 46.2 (March/April 2017).

"Interview by Rob McCellan: Seven Questions for Julie Carr": *Touch the Donkey, TtD supplement* (2014). http://www.touchthe donkey.blogspot.ca/2014/08/ttd-supplement-7-seven-ques tions-for.html.

"Interview by Sofi Thanhauser": *Entropy* (June 7, 2016). https:// entropymag.org/sofi-thanhauser-with-julie-carr/.

Someone Shot My Book

It is the dilemma or double bind of undertaking to put
the . . . elusiveness of signification in touch with political
responsiveness, in shifting contexts of social suffering and
affliction, political death and displacement, where life
reaches its limit. Of course, it is the limit that creates the
event of life, that is the necessary condition for the experi-
ence of life.
    —Athena Athanasiou[1]

In any case a poem (a poet) is always an uncomfortable
and threatening being who belongs equally to the cham-
bers of the living and the dead.
    —Chus Pato[2]

1. Bullet

Someone took my book out into the woods and shot it.[3] The
book is intimate with violence now in at least two ways—both
as subject matter (violence is what it's about) and as target. The
book reaches the gun as its interlocutor. Or, now the book, with
holes throughout, needs to be written again.

But when someone shot my book, I felt it got what it de-
served, that it had met its precise right audience. And I felt the
book had received its precise right author. The book had been
re-authored, or finally authored, by the bullet.

In aiming to silence life, the gun makes life more present; it
makes available, quite literally brings to hand, the grief we are
already feeling, the grief that one could call the precondition of
living. I don't mean to trivialize or exaggerate. But in trying to
understand what guns might give us, why some of us want them

so badly, I turn to this: in intimacy with death, in close proximity to grieving, is where we find ourselves most alive. *It is the limit that creates the event of life that is the necessary condition for the experience of life.*

"I propose to consider a dimension of political life that has to do with our exposure to violence and our complicity in it, with our vulnerability to loss and the task of mourning that follows, and with finding a basis for community in these conditions," writes Judith Butler in her important 2004 essay, "Violence, Mourning, Politics."[4]

Butler's venture: the just community could only be one that consistently recognizes—that does not banish—vulnerability, fear, grieving, those states that in attempting to deny we only become more and more subject to.

"Loss and vulnerability seem to follow from our being socially constituted bodies, attached to others, at risk of losing those attachments, exposed to others, at risk of violence by virtue of that exposure," she continues—a precise description of social life, I think, though mostly we attempt to locate ourselves outside of loss, refusing exposure.[5] Perhaps what guns seem to promise (to some) is to bring us closer, by way of the metonymic power of the object, to our actually lived vulnerability. Despite the claim that guns protect, we know that a person carrying a gun or a person with a gun in their house is far more at risk of death or injury than one who is unarmed, just as a society that is rich with guns is a society rich with risk.[6] I don't want here to rehearse the numbers. Rather, I want to consider the position of the one who is armed. For it seems only true that if I own a gun, I not only know that I could hurt you, but I also acknowledge that you could hurt me. As much as the symbol of a gun might seem to project power, it also suggests deep vulnerability. As one senator said to me during a hearing on gun control bills: "I assume everyone I meet is armed." The one who assumes this lives in fear, close to grief.

I'd like to say then, perversely, that the gun and the poem share a common purpose. And that purpose is to allow us these proximities.

2. Alert and Awake

Think of the mass killings in our country that have occurred in places we might consider sacred: the church, the temple, the school, the theater, the dance club. These places are not simply "public," they are, or were, places reserved for peace and communion, heartbreakingly figured by the Emanuel prayer circle in Charleston, South Carolina. In entering these spaces we remove ourselves from the chaos and struggle associated with the street or the marketplace as well as from the privacy of the home. This temporary shelter shared with others, often others we do not know, offers the promise of the common world that Hannah Arendt refers to as "the political," for they are spaces of conversation, contemplation, imagination, and pleasure—the groundwork of critique and of action. The killings that have happened in these spaces, then, don't so much as break into this sacred space as they reveal it as already broken. They reveal to us that the losses we experience were already in place, waiting to happen. The sense of sacred space is, we now know better, an illusion. As the NRA likes to remind us, there truly is no "gun-free zone." The killer we might have once thought excluded from these spaces enters them in order to show that such exclusion is a lie we've told ourselves. For the killer, there is no "outside," no ban—he is present, included everywhere.

In this sense, the act of killing exposes the fundamental lack of borders, the failure of demarcation, not just of the individual body but also of the so-called public sphere (which has always been marked by what it tries and fails to keep out). Maybe the increased insistence on the "right to bear arms" is at least in part an expression of an increased sense of boundary-less-ness that contemporary life has made acute. The gun, though seemingly a way to protect the limit of home or body, in fact reveals to us the "zone of indistinction" between public and private, between self and other, and between life and death. (It is important to note that the "right to carry" movement is not universally popular; rather, it is dominated by a specifically raced and gendered group—white males. See Chad Kautzer's "Good Guys with Guns: From Popular Sovereigny to Self-Defensive Subjectivity" for an analysis of what he calls "the emergent and pernicious form of political subjectivity in the United States—one which engenders equally problematic notions of freedom, security and sovereignty." Kautzer analyzes the crisis of white masculinity in contemporary America, reading the rapid increase of "right to carry" and "stand your ground" laws as a "legalization of non-state violence" and as symptomatic of that crisis.)[7]

The gun does not so much free its owner of this heightened vulnerability as it sharpens it, requiring or allowing the carrier to feel "alert and awake" at every moment. See the following advice from the website The Truth about Guns:

> Assuming that family safety is Job One, the all-important question becomes how, when and where might a life-threatening attack occur? The obvious answer . . . There is no way of knowing. The uncomfortable truth: family members and loved ones could be outside your care when an attack occurs. They could be with friends, at school, shopping, eating at a restaurant, driving—anywhere. Put that to one side. Where's the most likely place for a violent attack to occur when you're with your family? Again, who knows? You can't know if, when, where or how it will get real. The easiest way to cover the spread (as it were): carry a gun whenever you're with your loved ones. At the mall, soccer games, grocery shopping, wherever and whenever you gather. But especially at home—if only for one simple reason. You spend more time with your family at home than you do in any other physical location. So if it's going to happen someplace where y'all are, the odds are it'll be at home.
>
> It's also important to note that rapists, stalkers, psycho exes, disgruntled employees and other dangerous enemies know where to find you and your loved ones: at home.[8]

Another popular gun lover's website, Wide Open Spaces, offers ten reasons a person might want to carry a gun. This is reason number 9:

> Some people say that when they carry, they are more on edge
> and are better aware of their surroundings. When I carry, my
> senses are on high alert and I tend to know more of what is
> going on around me. Having a gun means I have to know
> what is happening.[9]

Since threat is everywhere, and most of all at home, there is no
moment that one should not be on "high alert." The presence
of the object (in your pocket) delivers you from your stupor.
Long ago (1800), William Wordsworth wrote of how blunted
the modern mind had become, so used to stimulus it no longer
cares to react, but rather sits passively in an almost "savage tor-
por." Poetry, he wrote, has the unique capacity to stimulate the
mind without the "violence" of so much of contemporary urban
life. Leap into modernism and you can find this again, such as in
I. A. Richards's *Science and Poetry* (1926), where Richards argues
for the labor of reading as a kind of stimulant that will draw us
from the "torpor" of the unfocused life, delivering us to "the
fullest, keenest, most active and completest kind of life."[10]

3. Distance and Proximity

> Revolutionary poetry may, exceptionally, have nothing at
> all to say about any fact that will be identified as political;
> its grammar may be thoroughly opaque and its sentences
> almost totally free of direct social reference. But impera-
> tively it must do this one thing: it must hurt and thrill a
> reader with an irresistible premonition of the feeling of
> being more fully and really alive than ever before, the
> feeling that is the true, unmistakable and inalienable basis
> of revolutionary subjective universality.
> —Keston Sutherland, "Revolution and Really Being Alive"[11]

In what we could call here, only half jokingly, the poetics of con-
cealed carry, Keston Sutherland (like Wordsworth and Richards
before him) calls on poetry to act on us the way the presence of
the gun acts on our NRA enthusiast: to awaken us into hyper-

awareness, to hurt us and thrill us into greater proximity with life.

But one can say, many have said, that awakening this "feeling of being more alive than ever before" is exactly what writing can *not* do, that writing is instead a form of estrangement, that in attempting to represent experience, writing kills experience. Even when turning away from mere representation or mimesis, even when poems try instead to *be* experiences, some will point out that poems (and all writing) always fall short. Whatever the experience one might have in having a poem, the argument goes, it's always at a remove from the "real," which would then have to be understood as pre-linguistic or sur-linguistic—as bodily and immediate.

And yet perhaps it's precisely in that failure, in the gap between the poem and "experience," that the poem matters most. I would venture that a poem can draw us nearer to our intensities, our desires and our grief, not because it describes such feelings with accuracy but because it does not. The gesture or attempt, the reach toward that is always falling short, is itself the moving element—which is why the single most resonant sentence about grief that I know is from Emerson writing on the death of his son: "I cannot get it nearer me."[12]

One could say that the root of social pain is this failure, but then so are the roots of social presence. To write is to approximate, to approach. The failure to arrive (at truth, at representation, at pure intimacy) moves us; effort and desire move us—as we become more aware of our longings, which is to say, our life. For the very reason that poetry fails to bring us our experiences of loss and vulnerability, it *is* loss and vulnerability.

The unsatisfiable desire that the poem represents, that the poem *is,* pays tribute to the ways in which I am not and never was self-possessed, not and never will be secure, to how I am instead and forever disarmed.

A fourteen-line poem on not giving up

1. A freckle between her shoulder blades
2. I keep trying to zip it
3. Have never

4. This system of marks, scrapes and wounds
5. Made palatable
6. On stage or screen or page
7. No no
8. But I wanted to be some kind of healer or farmer
9. Or else to be the wounded one
10. To make my mother cry
11. Desire achieves its lastingness
12. Pity narrative
13. Pity the body, these
14. Astringent bright blooms

"Only sheer violence is mute," said Arendt, who also posits that great speech and great action are coeval and coequal, belonging together in the realm of the political.[13] But if reasoned speech stands opposed to violence, poetic writing stands, instead, against it—leaning on it, the way we might lean against a wall. This is because unlike speech, the language of the polis, poetic language reaches toward the silence of grief, the muteness of violence. Poetic language lives in that failure, never hitting the mark. As poet Andrew Joron puts it, "where language fails, poetry begins." The poetic cry, he says, is "a triumph in defeat."[14]

4. Scar

"Poetry is a scar," writes Fred Moten on a number of occasions, pointing to the ways that poems tend to mark wounds, revealing the places we—as an individual or social body—are broken. "[Poetry] miscommunicates catastrophe in unseemly festivity," he says.[15] In his critical study *In the Break: The Aesthetics of the Black Radical Tradition*, Moten writes of the moment where "shriek turns speech into song." He finds one articulation of this moment in Frederick Douglass's *Narrative of the Life* where Douglass describes in close succession the shrieking of his Aunt Hester as she is being whipped and the "reverberation" of the "wild songs" sung by slaves who, in Douglass's words, consult "neither time nor tune." Douglass calls these songs "rude and incoherent,"

7

noting that even though he could not make out their words, they filled him with sadness, moved him to tears.[16]

A disturbed and disturbing form of communication aims at that which is disturbed or disturbing in the world, or in ourselves.

5. Mother

"There is nothing like the abjection of self to show that all abjection is in fact recognition of the *want* on which any being, meaning, language, or desire is founded," Kristeva wrote in 1980, anticipating Butler's description of the body as constituted precisely through its attachments, losses, and exposures.[17] In *Revolution in Poetic Language* (1977), Kristeva describes this "founding in want" as a phase in human psychic development she names the *chora*, both (or neither) a time and place, during which the pre-linguistic subject finds herself in a bodily, rhythmic "semiotic motility," regulated by and dependent upon the mother's body.[18] (Kristeva borrows the term from Plato's *Timaeus,* where it describes a receptacle or space, capable of transforming its character in response to whatever passes through—thus, associated with the mother.)

The developmental version of the *chora* precedes the so-called mirror stage in which the child begins to structure its identity through the symbolic order. But, crucially, Kristeva emphasizes that the semiotic *chora* is not a "stage" that is superseded or transcended; rather, its status is continual, in dialectic with the symbolic. As the symbolic's "precondition," it's also its twin.[19] While Lacanian theory posits, in Kristeva's words, that "dependence on the mother is severed, and transformed into a symbolic relation to an other," Kristeva argues for the *continued presence* of the pre-symbolic semiotic motility which finds its expression precisely in art, especially in poetic language.[20] It's in poetry (most acutely for Kristeva the modernist experimentation with language and form) that we can clearly see the *disruption* of the symbolic at play. Breaks in normative grammar, the overt use of rhythm and sound, syntactical disturbances, and the refusal or delay of semantic meaning all constitute the semiotic in language.

These are the literary devices that poets often call upon in defining their genre. But what's most distinct, and to me lasting, about Kristeva's take is that her semiotic is first and foremost a language of the body and of its drives, drives that are regulated through their dependence on an other. Their presence in the poem, then, is the mark of "abjection" or dependency, which Butler posits as a foundation for justice.

6. I/You

Unlike a poem whose object is absence (the missed or the missing), violence directs itself toward a presence, a seen (or, in the case of "precision guided munitions," *mapped*) object. And though it probably goes without saying that the perpetrator of violence is in some way confused about his or her desires, in the moment of enacting violence, the positioning of subject and object, the *grammar,* could not be more clear: I—hurt—you: subject—action verb—object.

"The thetic break" is Kristeva's term for the linguistic structure in this relation. Any statement (which is all statements) that insists on the position of the subject *as* subject is "thetic." The "thetic phase" of language acquisition establishes the speaker as a subject in relation to whom all other things and beings are objects. "There can be no language without a thetic phase" (72), admits Kristeva. And yet, in describing ritualized sacrifice as an extreme manifestation of the "thetic," she acknowledges the violent potential lurking in all structural relations where a subject acts upon an object. "The sacred—sacrifice—which is found in every society is, then, a theologization of the thetic," she writes in a chapter of *Revolution in Poetic Language* titled "Poetry That is Not a Form of Murder."[21]

And yet, as the title of that chapter indicates, Kristeva argues throughout *Revolution in Poetic Language* that not all language is in this way violent. Poetry answers to the violent face of the thetic by offering the ontological dislocation that opposes the thetic break: "poetic mimesis is led to dissolve not only the denotative function but also the specifically thetic function of *positing* the subject."[22] Poetic mimesis manages this dissolve of the thetic precisely because it works to dismantle the clear delineation of subject and object. This blurring of boundaries between I and you (experienced in the earliest relationship between mother and infant) is what Kristeva refers to with the term "jouissance":

> In cracking the socio-symbolic order, splitting it open, changing vocabulary, syntax, the word itself, and releasing from within them the drives born by vocalic or kinetic difference, jouissance works its way into the social and symbolic. In contrast to sacrifice, poetry shows us that language lends itself to the penetration of the socio-symbolic by jouissance, and that the thetic does not necessarily imply theological sacrifice.[23]

Not just an idea about language, Kristeva's semiotic/symbolic oscillation allows for an identity similarly oscillating between dependence and independence, between self-presence and abjection, and because of such uncertain founding, an identity in relationship not girded (only) by violence. That Kristeva locates the roots of this identity in maternity does not mean she necessarily fetishizes the maternal body. Rather, as Kelly Oliver has written, "Kirsteva uses maternity as an example of an experience that calls into question any notion of a unified subject. Maternity becomes a prime example of what [she] calls a 'subject-in-process.' . . . Kristeva analyzes maternity in order to suggest that all distinctions between subjects and objects, all identifications of unified subjects, are arbitrary."[24]

Butler's theory of identity, like Kristeva's (though less obviously), also draws on the early experience of dependency on a caregiver:

> I may wish to reconstitute my "self" as if it were there all along, a tacit ego with acumen from the start; but to do so would be to deny the various forms of rapture and subjection that formed the condition of my emergence as in individuated being and that continue to haunt my adult sense of self with whatever anxiety and longing I may now feel.[25]

"At one level, this situation is literally *familiar*," she writes. Pressing beyond the realm of psychic development (and not considering, as Kristeva does, ways in which this model of selfhood finds expression in language), as the War on Terror begins to define American life and life far beyond our borders, Butler asks us to resist the self-defensive subjectivity that she sees quite literally marching down the avenues.

Much more recently, in a conversation with Sarah Ahmed, she rearticulates the central question of the earlier essay:

> What if we shift the question from "who do I want to be?" to the question, "what kind of life do I want to live with others?" It seems to me that then many of the questions . . . about happiness, but perhaps also about "the good life"—very ancient yet urgent philosophical question—take shape in a new way. If the I who wants this name or seeks to live a certain kind of life is bound up with a "you" and a "they" then we are already involved in a social struggle when we ask how best any of us are to live.[26]

Kristeva too suggests the political potential of this recognition or "rapture" (jouissance), writing that only when the semiotic is present to disrupt symbolic signification and the division between subject and object that the symbolic expresses and enforces, only then, does "the signification process join social revolution."[27]

It seems clear that the turn away from emotional expression in poetry that with the advent of Conceptual Poetry made such headlines a few years ago (and what transformative years they have been), but which can be found in the digital poem's interest in pattern and process and traced to (some of) Language Poetry's rejection of subjective expression, was, when most sincere, actually an attempt to turn from destructive and potentially violent ideologies of subjectivity. Wanting the poem to belong to a collective, or to reflect social realities rather than "individual" ones, a poet or critic might valorize supposedly "desubjectivising" strategies, such as collage, appropriation, procedural, or documentary poetics (though all of these strategies can be mobilized for other reasons as well). Wanting to escape what seems like the bind of the ego in order to comment on culture more broadly, a poet might also stridently avoid material too close to home, too burdened by feeling. However, as such, the arguments "against expression" represent a failure to recognize what other models of identity might be at work in poems that highlight or generate emotion. These arguments "against expression" hinge on what I consider to be a patriarchal concept of self and a limited idea of the political work emotion can do.

If selfhood is in fact a shared entity, a vector made and remade through its encounters, then its emotions are shared as well. And this means, quite simply, that the emotional experiences we might discover in reading poems, or might find in making them, are not "private"; they do not "belong" to their author like some abstract form of property she's trying to protect or sell. This does not, however, make emotions less valuable, less powerful, or less important. Rather, it makes them more so. The social source and aim of emotion *is* its agency, its politics, and its engagement. This is why emotion in poetry matters: not because it's mine but because it's ours.

7. No Longer Alone

While gun ownership might in fact reach toward a (distorted) version of the vulnerability that Butler and Kristeva theorize as central to the building of something we could call, without shame, community, the gun carrier's sense of that vulnerability requires not that he *mourn*, the crucial second term in Butler's essay title, but that he redraw the boundaries of his corporeal self, his "family," or perhaps his social group. The carrier projects his losses, but among them is not the autonomy of the body itself. "There is no such thing as the human," writes Athanasiou, "instead, there is only the dizzying multiplicity of the cut human, the human body as interminably cut, fractured. In the clefts of history and at the limits of representation, the cut body of humanity tells the story of the indeterminability that haunts the dreams and nightmares of the 'fully there.'"[28] Therefore, despite what I read as the gun carrier's desire (shared with the poet) to be awakened into increased aliveness and charged affective attachment to others, the "self-defensive subject" (Kautzer's term) in insisting on being "fully there" reaffirms the thetic. And if rather than performing the decisive grammar of the thetic from the position of subject, the gun owner finds (as often happens) the bullet returned to his own body, then he will discover finally how bidirectional thetic violence truly is.

But the problem for the poet, a problem shared by anyone who seeks to create what Athanasiuou calls a "haptic technology," a generator of empathy, is how to deny our protections, how to stand exposed when difference and separation seem to mark the human body, in a society "stratified and marked by group conflict,"[29] where the threat of exposure seems to open us to the unbearable. For the most vulnerable people in our culture, those who are quite literally attacked (and today I am thinking of the trans woman, the black male, the poor, though now in Trump's America there are so many targets), the question seems almost perverse. "The problem, then, remains," writes Athanasiou, "how to think representation (cultural, political, textual) without the ontological presuppositions of authoritarian self-presence; how to think the body beyond the 'ontic,' beyond the representational presuppositions of the birth to presence; how to think the political beyond sovereignty; and, finally, how to think the language of the political beyond denomination."[30]

Poetic language, when most activated, thinks through these questions by way of threading shriek into word, cry into articulation. A poem will not stop a bullet, but it might, in this way, answer it—not heal a loss but draw attention to the losses we carry. As Nathaniel Mackey has written, poetry, "if not exactly a loser's art, is fed by an intimacy with loss and may in fact feed it."[31]

When the book met the bullet, it met the thing it was after and the thing that was after it: not its own death but its own life, made palpable through and in the broken face that was now its cover.

Notes

1. Athena Athanasiou, "Technologies of Humanness, Aporias of Biopolitics, and the Cut Body of Humanity," *Differences: A Journal of Feminist Cultural Studies* 14.1 (Spring 2003): 127.

2. Chus Pato and Erin Moure, *Secession/Insecession* (Toronto: Book Thug, 2014), 149.

3. Thank you to Nick Gulig for reading the book with a pellet gun.

4. Judith Butler, *Precarious Life: The Powers of Mourning and Violence* (New York: Verso Books, 2004), 19.

5. Ibid., 20.

6. According to a recent study conducted by a team of researchers at the University of Pennsylvania, people who carry guns are 4.5 times more likely to be shot and 4.2 times more likely to get killed as compared with unarmed citizens. The researchers looked at 677 shootings over two and a half years in Philadelphia to discover whether victims were carrying at the time and compared these victims to other Philadelphia residents of similar age, sex, and ethnicity. The team also accounted for other potentially confounding differences, such as the socioeconomic status of the neighborhoods. C. C. Branas et al., "Investigating the Link Between Gun Possession and Gun Assault," *American Journal of Public Health* 99.11 (2009): 2034–40.

7. Chad Kautzer, "Good Guys with Guns: From Popular Sovereignty to Self-Defensive Subjectivity," *Law Critique* 26 (2015): 173–74, doi:10.1007/s10978–015–9156-x.

8. "Guns for Beginners: Three Reason You Should Home Carry a Handgun," The Truth about Guns, accessed May 24, 2017, wwwthe ruthaboutguns.com.

9. "10 Reasons Why You Should Consider a Concealed Carry," Wide Open Spaces, accessed May 24, 2017, http://www.wideopenspaces. com/10-reasons-consider-a-concealed-carry.

10. I. A. Richards, *Poetries and Sciences, A Reissue of Science and Poetry (1926, 1935) with Commentary* (New York: W.W. Norton, 1972), 38.

11. Keston Sutherland, "Revolution and Really Being Alive," accessed May 24, 2017, http://sro.sussex.ac.uk/40496/1/Revolution_and_re ally_being_alive2_%281%29.pdf.

12. Ralph Waldo Emerson, "Experience," Emerson Central, accessed May 24, 2017 http://www.emersoncentral.com/experience.htm.

13. Hannah Arendt, *The Human Condition* (Chicago: University of Chicago Press, 1998), 26.

14. Andrew Joron, *The Cry at Zero* (Denver, CO: Counterpath Press, 2007), 1, 5.

15. Fred Moten, *Stolen Life* (Durham, NC: Duke University Press, 2018), n.p.

16. Fred Moten, *In the Break: The Aesthetics of the Black Radical Tradition* (Minneapolis: University of Minnesota Press, 2003), 20.

17. Julia Kristeva, *The Powers of Horror: An Essay on Abjection,* trans.

Leon Roudiez (New York: Columbia University Press, 1992), 5. Early on, Butler critiqued Kristeva's theory of the semiotic as failing to truly subvert the hegemony of the symbolic, as naturalizing the cultural proscription of motherhood, and as pathologizing lesbianism. Butler asserts (in 1989) that in Kristeva's theory "the semiotic is invariably subordinate to the symbolic." Judith Butler, "The Body Politics of Julia Kristeva," *Hypatia* 3:3 (Winter 1989): 105. See also *Gender Trouble: Feminism and the Subversion of Identity* (New York: Routledge, 2006), 101–18.

18. Julia Kristeva, *Revolution in Poetic Language*, trans. Leon Roudiez (New York: Columbia University Press, 1984), 46.

19. Ibid., 50.

20. Ibid., 48.

21. Ibid., 78.

22. Ibid., 58.

23. Ibid., 79–80.

24. Kelly Oliver, *Reading Kristeva: Unraveling the Double Bind* (Bloomington: Indiana University Press, 1993), 9.

25. Butler, *Precarious*, 26–27.

26. Sarah Ahmed, "Interview with Judith Butler," *Sexualities* 19.4 (2016): 10, accessed May 24, 2017, doi: 10.1177/1363460716629607.

27. Kristeva, *Revolution*, 61.

28. Athanasiou, 125.

29. Chad Kautzer, "Insurgent Subjects: Hegel, Césaire, and the Origins of Decolonial Phenomenology," in *Phenomenology and the Political*, ed. Geoffrey Pfiefer and West Gurley (Lanham, MD: Rowman & Littlefield, 2016), 3.

30. Athanasiou, 128. In a society that invests well over 50 percent of its discretionary budget on its military, with a gun industry pulling 13.5 billion dollars in revenue each year, the problem remains: how to create an economy of peace?

31. Nathaniel Mackey, "Sound and Sentiment, Sound and Symbol," in *Discrepant Engagement: Dissonance, Cross-Culturality and Experimental Writing* (Cambridge: Cambridge University Press, 2009), 36.

The Witch's House

A Poetics

And there is no place on earth for the mother.
—Kaja Silverman[1]

Sometimes when people write a poetics they begin by talking about war. Ron Silliman's *The New Sentence* begins that way. Williams's introduction to *The Wedge*. A war is hiding within Wordsworth's preface to *Lyrical Ballads*. A war stands behind Adorno's "Lyric Poetry and Society." From our time, Andrew Joron's "The Emergency," Kazim Ali's "A Brief Poetics: to Layla Al-Attar": each rests on the foundation of war.

Instead, I will talk about birth, that other epic. I will not say, however, that writing a poem is like giving birth or that the poem is like a child. The poem has no body. It's lighter than air. It can be allowed to die. When Plath writes in "Morning Song," "The clear vowels rise like balloons" she is and is not speaking of the baby's cries. Notice that she uses the article "The" rather than the possessive "Your," though she is speaking to the baby throughout the poem. A baby's cries are solid and demanding; they demand the mother's body. But the vowel sounds in the poem, these can drift upward, can belong to another realm— not another "world," for it is not a world. "The poem gestures off screen to where the world is happening, then back to the happening of the poem, where the world is a sounding of one noun after another."[2]

"I foam to wheat," Plath writes in "Ariel." The desire (as in many of Plath's poems) is to escape the solidity of earth—to escape it into the foam or froth of language. But the paradox is there; just as the clear vowels are not, but also are, the baby's cries, to escape the world is also to enter it: to foam to wheat.

Birth is a movement into the world and, for the mother, a tethering to the world through the body of the infant. However, birthing brings one into a strange proximity with death, or better put, life's absence. Birthing once was, and sometimes still is, very concretely close to death because so many mothers and infants did die in the process. But even when birthing poses vastly fewer risks, in the moment of giving birth one must confront the boundary between here and nowhere. One confronts this boundary not intellectually or metaphorically, but physically, psychically, entirely. The mother's body *is* that boundary. Anne Carson writes, "Woman is that creature who puts the inside on the outside,"[3] or, one could say, moves absence into presence, delivers nonbeing into being. (I'm finding it startling that we have no word for the state of nonliving that precedes life. We can only describe it in negative terms: nonbeing, nowhere, nothing. The three-year-old asks, "Where was I before I was born?" and we can only say, "Inside your mother," as a way to describe the time when she was not. So the mother carries a nothing, a nothing that becomes.)[4]

The poem, therefore, is not like the infant, with its clear and absolute demands. Rather, the poem resembles the birthing mother. The poem resembles her not because it "expresses" something that originates from within, not because it makes the private life of the poet into a public document, though some say that poems do these things. The poem as a thing made of words (what Hannah Arendt calls the "least dead" of dead things) resembles the woman in the act of birthing because it also could be said to stand at the border between being and nonbeing. Of the world, formed out of a language's responses to the world, the poem nonetheless stands outside of the world, caring and not caring—a sur-real object that circulates.

Here: two lives. In the first, practical life, you feed the kids. You do many other things, but all these other things are pointing in one direction—toward feeding the kids. This applies even if you don't have kids by way of extension or abstraction, for feeding the kids is a metonym for caring for the body, for the continuation of the human, of yourself as a human. In the other

17

life, you are removed from this task of feeding the kids—granted a reprieve. "Whim" on the lintels of the doorposts (Emerson), you're not home. Michael Palmer: "Words say, Misspell and misspell your name / Words say, Leave this life."[5]

In an article I once read about schizophrenia, the author described one woman's encounter with the disease as living always with the question of whether she is "here" or "not here." The person who is "here" is feeding the kids. The person who is "not here" might be writing a poem, might be living, instead, in the poem. (I don't mean to make a glib parallel between mental illness and poetry, but only to recognize that I recognize the question: here or not here?)

The poem doesn't "make a world." It makes a non-world. The world exists as a series of demands on one's body. One's body must respond to its own needs, to the needs of others, to spatial arrangements and to sensory experiences. But the poem exists only as marks on a page or as sounds in a room. But what then does a poem make? Dickinson says, "we live by the quaffing / bee and I." "Where the bee sucks, there suck I," says Ariel. Writes Keats, "thereby / Stood a cool vessel of transparent juice, / Sipped by the wander'd bee, the which I took." But if the poet is a bee, she is, as Rilke said, a maker of only invisible honey. "We perpetually gather the honey of the visible world in order to store it in the great golden hive of the invisible one."[6] Poets draw from the visible world to make something that does not finally resemble that world.

Mallarme: the poet "yields the initiative to words, through the clash of their ordered inequalities; they light each other up through reciprocal reflections like a virtual swooping of fire across precious stones."[7]

And yet, in the end, it is that very clash of inequalities, that movement of light, which draws our attention back to the source, which is the world itself. Here is Williams: "Look / for the nul // that's past all / seeing // the death of all / that's past // all being."[8] If the poem is that "nul" that realm beyond the visible, it nonetheless rhymes with the "all" as its twin.

Again Palmer: "Singing first the *solemn, imaginary* / world of brilliant error / recognized / as twin to the paradise / against which day breaks."[9] In that difficult twinning of language and world, of null and all, foam and wheat: that's where the poem is most alive.

2.

"'What is to become of us? How can we feed our children when we have nothing for ourselves?' says the poor woodcutter to his wife."

In Grimm's version of the tale, it is not absolutely clear that the wife is not also the mother of these children. In the first edition of 1812, she is called only "mother." In the final edition of 1857, either "mother" or "stepmother." In both, she is more often referred to simply as "the woman," arbiter of life and death, no less so than the witch in the house made of food. (In what follows I'll be quoting from the 1857 edition.)

"'Man, do you know what?' answered the woman. 'Early tomorrow morning we will take the two children out into the thickest part of the woods, make a fire for them, and give each of them a little piece of bread, then leave them by themselves and go off to our work. They will not find their way back home, and we will be rid of them.'"

"'No, woman,' said the man. 'I will not do that. How could I bring myself to abandon my own children alone in the woods? Wild animals would soon come and tear them to pieces.'

'Oh, you fool,' she said, 'then all four of us will starve. All you can do is to plane the boards for our coffins.' And she gave him no peace until he agreed."

The woman in this tale, as in so many, is the regulator and distributor of food. Fairytale wives, mothers, and witches feed, or do not, and when they do feed, they often poison. Blanchot writes (with more than a tinge of misogyny) of the "very remarkable passion of certain women who become poisoners: their pleasure does not lie in causing suffering, nor even in killing slowly, bit by bit, or by stifling, but rather it lies in reaching the indefiniteness that is death by poisoning time."[10] The figure of "woman" is, in our mythologies, the mark of this indefiniteness, standing not just on, but *as*, the fissure between the living and the dead.

In the tale of the children cast out into the woods, the father may have doubts, but in the end he is secondary, powerless to decide their fate. But in choosing their death, in choosing not to feed the children, in standing at the border between survival and death, is she, "the woman," the tale's poet?

"It was already the third morning since they had left the father's house. They started walking again, but managed only to go deeper and deeper into the woods. If help did not come soon, they would perish. At midday they saw a little snow-white bird sitting on a branch. It sang so beautifully that they stopped to listen. When it was finished it stretched its wings and flew in front of them. They followed it until they came to a little house. The bird sat on the roof, and when they came closer, they saw that the little house was built entirely from bread with a roof made of cake, and the windows were made of clear sugar."

When Hansel and Gretel are truly lost, have almost given up hope, they are saved not because they stumble unwittingly upon the house (as I'd remembered it) but because a bird sang. The bird, then, might be the poet, delivering the children toward what seems to be an answer, a miraculous solution—a world in which there is no more hunger. But, of course, the poet in this tale is not the bird, for though the bird sings, it has no words. It's the witch who speaks the first poem of the story:

Nibble, nibble, little mouse,
Who is nibbling at my house?

And the children respond to the poet/witch with a poem of their own:

The children answered:
The wind, the wind,
The heavenly child.

In this moment of poetry (because of irony, metaphor, and repetition), they recognize that in entering this new space they will become like wind, removed from the world, above the world. Like Plath's rising vowels, their cries will not be those of hunger but those of song: the song of the "heavenly child." But, as we know, the woman who feeds them is also the woman who would eat them. The poem might seem to deliver us, but if so it also removes us from ordinary life. Which is not, in the end, what we, or the children, want. When the children return home to their father, there is life, food, but no more "woman," no more poet (no witch/mother). But then the narrator of the tale, who has been until now silent, suddenly intrudes:

My tale is done,
A mouse has run.
And whoever catches it can make for himself from it a large,
    large fur cap.

This strange ending reminds us that the end of the tale always leaves something uncaught—there's always something that escapes the story, and that something here is a poem. If in the story we have returned to feeding the kids, the poetry within the story still evades that task. No mouse would provide enough fur for a "large, large fur cap," so of course this last line is ironic, or sardonic, pointing to the want that the story does not fulfill. In choosing to end on a poem, the "tale/tail" (or tale's tail) escapes the mundane, the domestic and all demands for food and clothing, for utility.

Orpheus's gifts of music and song come from his mother(s); he's the son of the Muses. But he's destroyed by women too, first drawn into death, then, when he escapes that, literally torn apart. The poem, then, is that border between being and nonbeing, the door of the little house—or perhaps of the oven itself: making life and taking it away.

Notes

1. Kaja Silverman, *Flesh of My Flesh* (Palo Alto, CA: Stanford University Press, 2009), 81.

2. Elizabeth Willis, "Bright Ellipses: Botanic Gardens, Leaves of Grass, and Meteoric Flowers," unpublished version, n.p.

3. Anne Carson, *Men in the Off Hours* (New York: Vintage, 2001), 4.

4. <u>A fourteen-line poem called Cry, baby</u>

1. So stripped of goals I had to lie down and cry
2. Or begin again with methods and strategies refined
3. I loved all my teachers and one by one they all died
4. I used the seven of spades as a bookmark
5. Just where the author admits to incest
6. We were in the psychodrama of nonviolence training
7. When we walked into the sea, hand in hand, the cops followed us
8. Seawater flowing into their guns
9. Now a cloudy morning, just where the author asserts his commitment to the self
10. For a long time it seemed the self was anathema
11. But after sovereignty and surveillance had their way with us, we had to return the individual to the scene
12. Her nipples and her cunt, and also her eyes
13. This was "the bad neighborhood of real life" in which the female body wears its insides on the outside
14. That was how we wanted her, wasn't it?

5. Michael Palmer, "Baudelaire Series," in *Codes Appearing: Poems 1979–1988* (New York: New Directions, 1988), 164.

6. Rainer Maria Rilke, *The Letters of Rainer Maria Rilke, Vol. II: 1910–1926*, trans. Greene Jane Bannard (Leiserson Press, 2007), 374.

7. Stephen Mallarme, "Crisis in Verse," in *Divagations*, trans. Barbara Johnson (Cambridge, MA: Belknap Press, 2007), 208.

8. William Carlos Williams, *Paterson* (New York: New Directions, 1992), 77.

9. Palmer, *Codes*, 59.

10. Maurice Blanchot, *Gaze of Orpheus and Other Literary Essays*, trans. Lydia Davis (Barrytown, NY: Station Hill Press, 1995), 85.

By Beauty and By Fear
On Narrative Time

1. Fear

"A window," writes Cole Swensen in the book I'm reading, "is a mode of travel . . . flying sleeves."[1] But here, gray rectangles of gray dawn—nothing more, nothing moves. Still in the bed, having slept hardly at all. A homemade dollhouse mocks me with its cardboard beds and paper rugs. A plaster wedding cake on the floor, a jumble of heels and skirts.

Back in the library sits a cart of photography books, each more gruesome than the last. I told the librarians I was researching violence and am embarrassed by how seriously they took me. In fact, I am researching my own fears. Every childhood is marked by qualities, and though I'm not proud of this, the quality I recall most often is that of fear. I had nothing too obvious, nothing too bodily, to fear. Nonetheless, most of my earliest memories, and many of those that follow, are memories of fear.

The vines at the window, the threads that unraveled from the blanket, the cats I lived with, the fireplace, and the dark wood of the floor. The cold at my wrists in winter, the heat against my eyes in summer. Smells from the sidewalks. Any ball in the air. Any dog not tied. The girls across the street. The boys. The cupboards and the backs of drawers. My brother's hands and my mother's mouth.[2]

Insomnia plagues the fearful.

"What is it to be a *who* or a *me*, or even more radically, a *no one*: without identity, that is, no longer able to say 'I'?" asks Gerald

Bruns in *On Ceasing to Be Human,* where he examines various claims of non-self-identity that run through twentieth-century European philosophy. Sleep, he argues, offers precisely the escape from the self that is both longed for and feared.[3] Sleep—the house of the unnarratable I.

Bruns has also written on Wordsworth's fear, here in the line from *The Prelude* I've borrowed to title this essay. And for Bruns, the fear Wordsworth explores throughout *Lyrical Ballads* and also in *The Prelude* is less the fear of not being an *I* than that of becoming another: "the fear that intimacy with another mind carries with it [is] a risk of transformation into the strange, the monstrous, the more-or-less-than . . . human."[4] To encounter the monstrous in a book, in the streets, or in your mother is to experience the terror that one might become, one might in fact already be, this one who murders, this one who raves.

I could not sleep because of fear, because the year I spent reading websites and staring at photography books that featured some of the most monstrous things humans do to others was also the year my mother shat in the furnace room when she could not find the bathroom, the year she wandered the house sobbing "miserable, miserable" to herself or to us. The year I lost her to miserable was the same year I spent in the archives of American violence, as if one set of fears might outshine another. Of course I feared losing her to misery. Of course I also feared losing myself, to her misery or to my own, or to the misery that is all of ours—a particular American misery. Perhaps not sleeping became a way to protect, with avid intensity, the fiction of the coherent narratable self, this temporary invention of the day.

> Calm succumbs to the hour . . . An embedded immensity fills
>   you . . .
> There is no self just this falling off

Claudia Rankine speaks over the faces John Lucas has filmed, the soft faces of people asleep on planes, sky drifting past. Rankine calls sleep "the inevitable move inward" but inward toward what, if in sleeping I "lose myself"? "Isn't this confidence? / Isn't this the completed life?" she asks as they float.[5]

At fifteen in an airport alone I picked up a payphone to call my friend Kate. She answered from a room in which she and her parents and brother had just learned that her other brother, the other twin, had been killed. A room: from Latin "rus," or "open land." I hung up the phone and redirected myself into that room where unpoured Coke and Sprite sat gleaming in candlelight. Kate's mother with her hand at her mouth. Everyone looking at nothing but the floor. That floor, that open open.

And now, decades later, another friend from that time—she's the one staring at nothing. An SUV jumped the curb where she was walking with her two sons. The older one, ten, a slight boy with dimples in his grin, was struck and taken. In another airport, some dim hallway, I stand trying to breathe, my forehead against a carpeted wall. TSA workers kindly pass me by.

Ever since I started to track it, I watch from the distance of intact motherhood the parade of parents whose faces we fear for fearing we will wear them.

Some deaths are accidents, some are not, some accidents are lies, some lies deemed legal, some laws criminal.

"We are all (at some time or another) observing a deathwatch over our mother," wrote Derrida,

or a deathwatch over kids.

It's been said that poetry can reverse the movement of time— for when you get to the end of the line, you have to go back to the beginning again. "Our eyes darting from the end of one line to the beginning of another create a kind of instability in linear time," says Chris Nealon paraphrasing J. H. Prynne.[6] It's also been said that poetry ruptures time—makes a hole in the movement of time we call "day" or "hour." This happens when language is so thick and complex that to read is to get caught in traps and ruts. All those "little knots of impacted, concentrated, dense language: paradoxes, ambiguities, and indeterminacies; self-reference and repetition," writes Cathy Gallagher, " seem to cross back and forth over [themselves] and consequently to thwart forward movement."[7] Complexity and recurrence—more than literary devices—a refusal of directed velocity.

A poem, perhaps, is an anti-narrative, which might be a good reason to fear it:

> and so an instant can really get intense
> through forceful concentration
> forcefully knotted
>
> And its emotion is only rooted
> in the certainty of accident
>
> —Nicolas Pesques[8]

A swell of laughter from across the room: the conspiratorial laughter of colleagues. My mother, counting all her losses, the foremost among them, linear time, said that what she most longed for was a "colleague." It was hard for her to remember this word—but it was an important word, I realize now, because a colleague is that person who shares in your process of narrating the self. A colleague assists you in making a fiction, a fictional self. A family member's intimacy reveals the failures of that fiction. A family member knows too much about accident and error, and anyway, intrudes, makes a mess of you. Perhaps this is why telling your life story to people on buses and planes, your passing, temporary colleagues, is such a drug.

2. Name

"How's the baby?" I ask. "Doing good, doing good. But he's doing that day/night reversal thing." Because the wind is blowing, we keep the conversation short. The baby's wrapped up but for his little face, his shut tight eyes. Clouds amassing in the west turn the blue sky dark. Babies are good, but they stay up all night. The wind is blowing. They haven't yet given him a name.

Why must the Queen in the fairytale, trying to save her baby, guess the little man's name? A name out of nowhere, an untraceable, unlocatable, unrootable nonsense name could never *be* guessed. It would be like trying to see a color that does not exist. Though the story says, "He took pity on her," on her maternal terror, it's obvious that by asking her to guess his impossible name he is showing her exactly no pity. But the Queen is no innocent either, for Kingly greed has infected her; once "humble, meek, and grateful," now, despite her promises, she's greedy for her child. And her greed directs her to cheat, to use her power, her servants, to find out the little man's name. She wins in the end, which means the baby wins his permanent home and eventual kingdom (for don't forget, this baby is the heir). But this winning is a result of deception, which is perhaps a fact of all kingdoms—won through lies, by way of lying, just as pity is a lie. A pretty pitiless tale.

The little man never thought for a moment that she'd guess his name (and he was right about that). He exposed himself, however, by the fire. Confessions—burned out of us as dance and song.

And yet, the name is not just a riddle that once solved will land the Queen safely in the country of mothers; it's also a curse, for once spoken it destroys the little man. He flies off through the window on a spoon and is "never heard from again," or, in the darker versions, he's so enraged he stamps a hole in the earth and is sucked down into it. Unbirthed: taken back into the body. The little man—the baby's doppelganger—is the unnamed one who must be destroyed in order to complete the narrative, in order to reinforce (patriarchal) order, which relies on names.

So what happens when my friends finally name the baby boy? Is something lost at that moment, even when so much is gained? Does the baby, in taking on a name, become, in some other way, swallowed? Here's Blake:

"I have no name;
I am but two days old."
What shall I call thee?

"I happy am,
Joy is my name."
Sweet joy befall thee!

That verb "befall" hints at the crisis that circles the act of naming. The verb dates back to Old English (897) and seems to have meant simply "to fall" until the twelfth century, when it began to also mean "to inherit"—which is certainly one of Blake's meanings here. But as I search the OED I find that almost all instances of "befall," where it takes an indirect object ("thee"), indicate an inheritance that is bad or dangerous—that will leave its object worse off, not better.

"I do not know what it gives," wrote H.D. of the "jewel" vibrating at the center of her poem "Tribute to the Angels": "a vibration that we can not name, // for there is no name for it; / my patron said, 'name it'; // I said, I can not name it, there is no name."[9] Patrons, kings, queens—need things named. Poets, though they trade in words (or because they do), recognize and defend the unnameable core that burns.

Before named, the infant of Blake's poem is pure happiness. Language can't even organize itself correctly around that happiness (I happy am). But once named, once "called," it suffers a fall, one could say, into narrative. No easy opposition, then, between the fear of no narrative and the comfort of having one. Because as soon as you begin to tell yourself, something of yourself is lost. And not all narratives, dear mothers and fathers, dear children, end well.

Cloud mounds. Heaps. Masses. And the little lifted screens click and hum. One could turn things off, but not the sky. One could read the entire newspaper start to finish. Start to finish. Mouth to foot. So I said to my head, go on. One could visit the green edges of the mind in cafés where one talks to oneself through the keys. There, on a rickety chair, a woman sat picking at her food and told me a story.

The last thing she said was, "He finished the job," as if we were in a movie.

The story is about a man who was sleeping on her mother-in-law's couch. Her mother-in-law was helping him out because he was having some troubles. They were both in Houston for a time, "finishing a job" in order to earn their pensions. The mother-in-law hadn't told anyone about the guy on her couch and, it seems, hadn't been aware that he was using. He was just a coworker, a friend, and he too had left his family behind to follow this job—his wife and five kids. Something about this story feels incomplete. Everything about this confession is borrowed. He killed her, says the woman across from me, with a kitchen knife. He stabbed her over nine times. "Finished the job."

The son, my friend's husband, makes plans to visit a firing range in order to learn how to shoot. This is perhaps a reasonable response. Perhaps not.

That night, I can't sleep. My head hurts and I'm awake at three. In the glow of the lamplight, I read two stories.

The first is narrated by a ghost. The ghost watches while a wealthy eccentric old man has sex with his (the ghost's) dead body. Because the ghost is beyond caring about his body, he empathizes with the old man's suffering and befriends him, listens to him through the night as the old man confesses to, and attempts to explain, his depravity.

In the second story, a boy witnesses the slow death of his older brother. The brother, dying of cancer, is nonetheless cruel and violent. And when he can no longer behave violently, he does so by proxy—has a friend hurl a padlock at his younger brother's face. What do these stories have in common? What do they share with the story told in the café? Depraved, sick, lonely, and lost boys and men. The standard situation for narratives.

"Let me in," say the women, picking at their food.

They named him Owen.

Once he is named he begins to have a face. Once he has a face, he will begin to make sounds other than instinctual. He will begin with vowels, and they will rise, as Plath said, like balloons.

Not sleeping might be an illness, or it might be a symptom. A product or a producer of fear. The unnamed little man at the fire will take your child. Only the vigilance of insomnia will allow you to hunt down his name, will keep your kid safe, and keep you too in the story. But after a number of weeks of not really sleeping, I begin to fear, not just the nights, but the days too.

3. Beauty

> Fair seed-time had my soul, and I grew up
> Fostered alike by beauty and by fear (*The Prelude*)

The beautiful and the fearful (or the sublime, as the mother of fear) are the two dominant aesthetic categories during Wordsworth's time. One might say his effort throughout *The Prelude* is to work out their relation. Fear, he suggests, turns its ear outward, listening for external threat:

> I heard among the solitary hills
> Low breathings coming after me, and sounds
> Of undistinguishable motion, steps
> Almost as silent as the turf they trod.
> . . .
> With what strange utterance did the loud dry wind
> Blow through my ear!

But beauty, it seems, when not referring to some transitory attribute of a girl, lad, or sky, wells up from within, is the mind's answer to sublime terror, the mind's imaginative ability to reorganize, or "harmonize"—to make coherent sense out of what it fears:

> Dust as we are, the immortal spirit grows
> Like harmony in music; there is a dark
> Inscrutable workmanship that reconciles
> Discordant elements, makes them cling together
> In one society.

Elsewhere Wordsworth calls beauty an "ennobling Harmony." But more famous and more bold is Wordsworth's triumph at the very end of Book XIV, where, having confronted the "fixed, abysmal, gloomy, breathing-place"—the earth, which he earlier refers to as "an enemy"—he now declares the mind of man "A thousand times more beautiful than the earth / On which he dwells." The mind, "in beauty exalted" imbued with imagination, spells the end of fear: "For there fear ends."[10]

But what if pulling beauty apart from sublime terror is not an option? What if beauty cannot tame fear, for the feared thing and the beautiful thing are one?

An older allegory serves me better: Hephaestus, the ugly forger of technologies, was in a rage against his beautiful wife's promiscuity. The net he wove of gossamer thin wire was meant to capture Aphrodite in the act of betraying him. But when he trapped her and her lover, the irascible and violent Ares, the other gods gathered around and only laughed and laughed.

That gossamer net forged with precision is one way to understand narrative. And beauty, which rises out of foam, defies the traps set for it. She has, as the story tells us, more affinity with violence than with the "inscrutable workmanship" of craft. According to Homer, the entrapment only leads Aphrodite to divorce Hephaestus, for in the *Iliad* she "consorts freely with Ares." And so beauty slips out of the grip of craft and into the arms of brutality.

Poetry, writes Blanchot, is in "sympathy with darkness, with aimless passion, with lawless violence, with everything in the world that seems to perpetuate the refusal to come into the world."[11] In sympathy with the unnameable magician dancing around the flames.

It's been said that our name is our first story; I learned to paint mine on an easel, steadying myself with letters. At that time the song I loved to sing most was "Michael Row Your Boat." I loved it, then, because of milk and honey and for the comfort of its names: Michael, Brother, Sister. I love it now for other reasons.

As in many of the African American spirituals, the words give instruction from slave to slave on how to access freedom, how to break out of the story that has been written for you: don't talk about it, don't boast, code it in song. The song or the poem creates a momentary erasable bridge when the structural bridge is not there and is too dangerous or impossible to build. "In the end what I'm interested in is precisely that transference, a carrying or crossing over, that takes place on the bridge of lost matter, lost maternity, lost body and its ephemeral if productive force," writes Fred Moten reading Frederick Douglass reading slave song.[12]

Michael's boat's a music boat: the fragile, temporary, wild-built beauty of song set loose in a four-year-old mind that knows nothing yet of the stolen lives that made that song and sings it not to taste that bitterness but to taste something sweet, something luxurious, tasting the bitter nonetheless.

269.
Wild Nights—Wild Nights!
Were I with thee
Wild Nights should be
Our luxury!

I read that too once I could read. And it's Dickinson who said of beauty, "Chase and it ceases"; like wind in the grasses, you can't overtake it. Fear she called a stimulus, an impetus, and a spur. One draws you forward, the other pushes you from behind, but it's that same wind on either side. Put your boat into that wild storm: "Done with the Compass— / Done with the Chart!"— that Eden.

Once I started sleeping again and found myself an ordinary person, riding buses and drinking coffee, standing around in a singular body in that endless Denver sun, I was stunned by my own presence, its bright dailyness. Sidewalks felt hard again under my feet, the air sharper, my senses were re-revealed. That sounds emotional. It was, but it was also physical. One morning the sky was all Easter, so pink and salmon, so baby blue, I thought it must be kidding. Going for a walk, making a meal, it all seemed obscene. Obscene because what had scared me, my mother's misery, the country's misery behind and before the gun, these twin terrors, had gone nowhere, they only got worse. But I was back to belonging because I had to be, or because I could be, and it did and didn't seem alright.

There really is no poem outside of fear, no sublime on one page and beauty on the other. To write is to call to that fear, to lie down in it. Or to put it more bluntly, the terror of the un-narratable, un-nameable "I" that I encounter in my mother's mind full of holes, is fucking the beauty I want—the anarchic violent poem.

So I end with and in my mother again, who raged out of fear and feared her rages and who now, with no narratives left ("discarding the ceremony of consciousness / drifting into nothing"), is, one could say, no longer a mother—who, without linear time, can no longer scare me and no longer love me. And if she's no longer a mother, than I'm no longer a child—now a dead child. But maybe emotions, once set into action, continue indefinitely like entropic molecules, even after the person who "felt" the emotion can no longer "feel" it or say it or know it. Perhaps love stands outside of narrative, antagonistic to story—like language, just something people walk into, row out into. Is love, then, a condition rather than a feeling? Like language, a condition, not of the person but of the world?

Notes

1. Cole Swensen, *The Glass Age* (Farmington, ME: Alice James Books, 2007), 10.
2. A fourteen-line poem on having once been a child

1. I hate my desktop and my homepage
2. Back when I was a child: three overlapping worlds
3. Sequins on a windowsill
4. Unrestrained futurism: like a hard cock with no conscience
5. I dream of a huge swimmer in the
6. alien air, dream
7. the emerald platters clatter
8. in the whistle of a disco
9. Serial cereals this and every
10. morning's marvel: my baby's been made
11. a man, I'm not
12. done

13. There lies the melodious rage of the garage
14. Worker's wheels, so slowly now

3. Gerald Bruns, *On Ceasing to Be Human* (Palo Alto, CA: Stanford University Press, 2010), 3.

4. Gerald Bruns, *Hermeneutics: Ancient and Modern* (New Haven, CT: Yale University Press, 1995), 171. It should be noted that Wordsworth's others are marked primarily by poverty, monstrous to him for the affliction of not having as often as they are afflicted with madness or sorrow.

5. Claudia Rankine and John Lucas, "Situation 2," accessed May 24, 2017, http://claudiarankine.com.

6. Christopher Nealon,"The Prynne Reflex," accessed May 24, 2017, http://theclaudiusapp.com/4-nealon.html.

7. Catherine Gallagher, "Formalism in Time," *MLQ* 61.1 (March 2000), 247.

8. Nicolas Pesques, *Juliology*, trans. Cole Swensen (Denver, CO: Counterpath Press, 2008), 6.

9. H.D., *Trilogy* (New York: New Directions, 1998), 76.

10. William Wordsworth, *The Prelude: A Parallel Text* (New York: Penguin, 1971): I:301–2; I:322–25; I:337–38; I:340–44; VII:771; XIV:30; XIV:449–50; XIV:454; XIV:163.

11. Maurice Blanchot, *The Work of Fire*, trans. Charlotte Mandell (Palo Alto, CA: Stanford University Press, 1995), 330.

12. Moten, *In the Break*, 18.

Spirit Ditties of No Tone
On Listening

> Hearing is full of doubt: phenomenological doubt of the
> listener about the heard and himself hearing it. Hearing
> does not offer a meta-position; there is no place where
> I am not simultaneously with the heard. However far its
> source, the sound sits in my ear.
> —Salome Voegelin[1]

> Listening . . . waits in the silence that fills the future lying
> all about the utterance.
> —Susan Stewart[2]

1.

Hearing and listening. What's the difference? We ask our chil-
dren to be "good listeners"; we don't mean that they should
have ears full of doubt, that sound should "sit in their ears." By
"listen" we mean, understand, and, if I am giving orders, obey.
Jean-Luc Nancy writes of the "slight keen indecision that grates,
rings out, or shouts between 'listening' and 'understanding': be-
tween two kinds of hearing . . . between a sense (that one listens
to) and a truth (that one understands), although the one, in the
long run, cannot do without the other."[3] Can one do without
the other? Roland Barthes begins his essay "Listening" with an
attempt to parse the difference between the physiological act
of hearing and the psychological act of listening.[4] What might
happen if we try, even for a moment, confronting language, to
foreground the former?

As usual I've been spending time listening to poets read,

but not only to their poems. Also, "my ear bends" to the things they say before, after, and between the poems, that unimportant language—its murmuring, hesitation, and rhythms. "OK, Charles, I'll just jump right in." Or, "This poem's speaker loves obsolescence." Listening too to academic talks, their particular banter: "pinching and elliptical grammar," says someone; "we're spinning out of emplotment," says someone else; "the standard view of modern science is a disarranged intellect that lacks an object"; "The triumphal narrative of the emergence of a rational-critical sphere." Lifted from context, each line traverses a rhythmic and sonorous landscape, which I try, with my ears, to "see."

Listening, writes Barthes, "is a mode of defense against surprise." Making sense of sound, we protect ourselves against the unknown. What if instead of defending, we were to court the surprise, the untranslated noise? What if we turn toward, or even create, what Susan Howe calls a "conscious phonemic cacophony" of found sound?[5]

While listening, I've been writing (there is no "while," really, I do one or the other), getting down every third word or so as I try to keep my writing in time with my listening. Writing what "sits in my ear," the heard sentences, produces new ones that bear a ghostly relation to their source, as if clothing without a body—all surface, no substance. Listening to "the blind sight of sound,"[6] I am looking for ways to escape the deliberations of thinking, to "spin out of emplotment," to become a "disarranged intellect," to move sound into an improvisatory mode. I want the physiological process, distilled, to get to an affective state I can't really name—perhaps *presence*.

"The reception of sound might be framed as a *feeling*," writes Susan Stewart, as if the act of hearing, and not the interpretation of the thing heard, is the source of emotion, as if "tuning the ear" is an affective act.[7] But it is, because the effort to take in sound as an abstraction forces me to become aware of the intense soundscape I'm always living inside of anyway but that I mostly ignore in an attempt to make sense of noise. Undifferentiated listening reveals the pure functioning of sensation, in other words, the welling up of living, of being alive.

In this land to which his mother is crossing over, no longer able to understand anything she once understood, she will no longer need any words, this much he understands. For one brief, sharp, clear moment, he understands what it would be like if he could arrive there along with her. . . . Briefly, sharply, clearly he knows for one instant what it would feel like if the audible and the inaudible, things distant and near, the inner and outer, the dead and the living were simultaneously there, nothing would be above anything else, and this moment when everything was simultaneously there would last forever. . . . But because he is a human being . . . this knowing free of language passes from him just as suddenly as it arrived.[8]

This passage occurs near the end of Jenny Erpenbeck's novel/meditation on death, *The End of Days*. Reading it, suspended thirty-six thousand feet above the earth, my little shade drawn, my row partner asleep, I realize with a shock that my effort to get through language to the beyond of language, to the pure sound of language, has been wrapped up in longing, in the wish to return to my mother, for whom language is now only sound, only sound and inflection, only feeling. Somehow I've been trying to hear how she hears, to be, in this way, *with* her.

But it's an imperfect practice. Suspended between its own preoccupations and its true availability to another's voice, another's sound, attention seems to hover. "The auditory . . . manages to trouble . . . the clear distinction between subject and object, inside and the outside, self and the world," writes Michael Bull.[9] I start calling this process *Think Tank:*

Injured fugitives from the markets generously ask for too
    little
I'm wishing for gardens and salty stars without context—
far too extravagant—and then the phone rings with a light
    of its own

Fog returns a catalogue

Pinching and elliptical grammar sits slightly tipped at the
    horizon. Huge invoices
    collapse in my eyes

Irresponsible and aimless, this is a white clock, a white
   cock and billowing flowers in ignorance tender, in igno-
      rance draw

   incoherent patterns through the candlelight[10]

"It is in the engagement with the world, rather than in its per-
ception that the world and myself are constituted," writes Voege-
lin. "The task" of engagement through listening, she goes on,
"is to suspend, as much as possible, ideas of genre, category,
purpose, and art historical context, to achieve a hearing that
is the material heard, now"—this is an engagement with sound
about as close to pure sensation as you can get.[11] But it's also a
practice. Voegelin is talking about listening to music, but words
too can be material sound, as they might be for a baby, or an ani-
mal, to my mother now. But to hear in this way, to hear openly,
requires a disciplined *dis-cernment* (from Latin meaning to un-
separate), that is, an un-judgment, an uneasy practice of mis-
understanding.

   Barthes considers such "open" listening an ethical practice:
"listening is *taking soundings* . . . what is plumbed by listening
is intimacy, the heart's secret: Sin."[12] To listen to another, in a
Catholic context as in a psychoanalytic one, is to commit to inti-
macy, to begin an attempt to heal the other, or oneself (confes-
sion understood, here, not as a prelude to punishment but as
the first step in healing). Pauline Oliveros also suggests a direct
connection between listening and compassion. Her "deep lis-
tening" is, as I understand it, a way of expanding the soundscape
one feels ready to acknowledge, thereby stretching the boundar-
ies of one's ability to "feel with."[13]

   Barthes explains that the ideal listener must not actively in-
terpret the thing heard, must "simply . . . listen and not trou-
ble to keep in mind anything in particular" (Freud, quoted in
Barthes),[14] but he acknowledges how readily the analyst/priest
will fail at this unadulterated absorption of sound. As Stewart
disappointingly reminds us: "sounds . . . are never heard outside
an expectation of meaning"; there is no *pure* listening, no *pure*
sound.[15]

But what about mystical theories of language, such as Walter Benjamin's concept of the "pure language" behind all languages?

> That which seeks to represent, to produce itself in the evolving of languages, is that very nucleus of pure language. . . . In this pure language—which no longer means or expresses anything but is, as expressionless and creative Word, that which is meant in all languages—all information, all sense, and all intension finally encounter a stratum in which they are destined to be extinguished.[16]

If verbal sounds are divided, however fleetingly, however imperfectly, from meaning, would that momentary "extinguishing" of intension and information reveal something of greater value, something *more*? The "critical question," writes scholar Susan Handelman responding to Benjamin, "is what is meant by that 'something more' that 'something else,' that 'abyss' or 'depth' in language that both mystics and poets sense and explore—a nihilistic void or a depth of divine mystery? Is the 'beyond' the negative abyss of all meaning and expression . . . or a higher, fuller realm of meaning?"[17] In a short piece called "The Dismemberment of Language" (published in 1928 and excerpted from his *Origin of the German Tragic Drama*), Benjamin writes admiringly of "words, syllables and sound emancipated from all traditional associations of meaning" in Baroque drama. In these plays, he writes, "The vocalized word is only haunted by meaning . . . as if by an inescapable illness."[18] The tonal and rhythmic aspects of language, their phonic substance, or what Octavio Paz called their "plastic" qualities, could generally be said to overwhelm their denotative meanings only when one is listening to a foreign language or to an unfamiliar discourse within one's own. Choosing, or practicing, such ignorance might seem a foolish, fruitless, and even futile mission. But with Benjamin I want to consider the work of the ear as its own kind of knowledge and the mind's habitual curtailment of sound as an ignorance.

While for Benjamin in "The Task of the Translator," literary works are never really about "information" ("For what does a literary work 'say'? What does it communicate? It 'tells' very little to those who understand it. Its essential quality is not communication or the imparting of information"),[19] translation, as an acute form of listening, might offer the distinct possibility of freeing words from their limits, for in bringing the untranslated word into the language at hand, the translator momentarily wrenches the word from its attachment to a habitual understanding. Before it arrives, in that moment before the translation has been chosen, there is a suspension, a hovering.

Liberated or healed, words might then become what Susan Howe (whose writing is so often between histories, between languages) calls a "nonsense soliloquy replete with transgressive nudges . . . a vocalized wilderness format of slippage and misshapen dream projection."[20]

In my active meditation on or *of* listening, I tried to delay or blur the expectation of understanding long enough to approach such wilderness in the present. In writing the poems whose primary intention was to access an affective state of pleasure (in sight, if not at the site, of love), I cajoled listening to tank thought. And yet, language's desire to narrate cannot be fully extinguished; it smolders in word order, which strains toward familiarity. In that tension between listening to language—to what Fred Moten calls the "phonoerotic" of sound—and translating such sounds into language once again burdened, even if lightly, by story, that's where writing happened.

> Spinning out of emplotment and derivative lexicon, sweet
> lexicon
> toward what lycanthropic dream?
>
> Was metal and declensional, a material
> Fem. Scattered my passwords in some dog-run dirt
>
> Loved nothing so much as a spot on his head
> as the valve in my wet
>
> snowbound
> day. Twinned twigs in plum tree win
>
> tears of sap

up from source-seeking low down

root. Morning's not
    measured nor meant
    just assured and rude in its lack of regard.

Euphonic rubber spin
who's driving you where
    why drink-in the warm air pressed from the
    dash dash dash

of your figurative folk-form my hap-
    hazard phrase is cued, lit, and moving

down the avenue, the avenue
8's
    just lesions all the way down[21]

2.

Poetry is . . . speech framed to be heard for its own sake
and interest even over and above its interest of meaning.
Some matter and meaning is essential to it but only as
an element necessary to support and employ the shape
which is contemplated for its own sake. (Poetry is in fact
speech only employed to carry the inscape of speech for
the inscape's sake . . .)
—Gerard Manley Hopkins, 1873[22]

For Hopkins, the "inscape" or sonic patterning of the language
is "supported" by meaning as a secondary element (this is the
reverse of how people commonly think about the relationship
between sound and meaning in poetry). Inscape manifests,
Hopkins explains, through the process of "oftening, over-and-
overing, aftering." In other words, through sound repetition we
reveal the supra-semantic play always lurking above or around
denotative language. That this surface-oriented poetics deliv-
ered pleasure to Hopkins is a claim I cannot make, given his

biography. However, certainly his early poems are aimed at joy, and, one can argue, a form of joy (a formal joy?) remains even in the "Terrible Sonnets," though their content, their "matter and meaning," is terror and grief.

> NO worst, there is none. Pitched past pitch of grief,
> More pangs will, schooled at forepangs, wilder wring.

Isn't there, in that "wilder wring," a kind of rich pleasure, a sounded intensity that can be heard or felt, if not thought? After all, it's thinking that causes the most pain to Hopkins: "Thoughts against thoughts in groans grind," he wrote in "Spelt for Sybil's Leaves,"[23] while the first lines of "Spelt" offer a tribute to the *ear* that is at the same time a love song to the *ear*th: "Earnest, earthless, equal, attuneable, vaulty, voluminous, . . . stupendous / Evening strains to be time's vast, womb-of-all, home-of-all, hearse-of-all night." I cannot *not* read "ear nest" in that "earnest," for, in fact, the ear is a kind of nest: a woven home for sound.

If the "pangs" of grief are intensified through repetitive or obsessive thinking, language's "pangs"—intensities of sound rather than moments of pain—deliver its ir-rational affective resonances. One could say that in Hopkins, even where we find most emotional suffering, we find exulted language, language exulting through and on its sonic surface. As Novalis, who seems to have had much in common with Hopkins, puts it, "One fails to comprehend language, because language doesn't comprehend itself, and doesn't want to comprehend itself. The true Sanskrit [i.e., the root language] speaks for the sake of speaking, because speaking is its passion and its essence."[24]

The "pitch" and "ring" of music in Hopkins's poems press against, and to my ear override, the overt narrative content—or, they invent another content that the poem and reader must admit. If Hopkins is pitched *past* grief (to another emotion, one he does not name, for maybe it has no name), language's surface pleasures get him there.

And yet, Hopkins could not entirely forego the narrative sentence and its pull into linear time—and, it should be said, he was wed to a larger teleological narrative too: that of Revelation. Of the poets since who have been able, in part because of Hopkins as forerunner (and not only because of Dada or Stein), to come much closer to loosening the pull toward semantic sense, I'll end with just one: Jackson Mac Low, chosen in part because of some autobiographical connections. When I was in my twenties I danced for a slew of Saturday mornings at the East Village's P.S. 122 with Mac Low's daughter Clarinda. We were part of an ad hoc group of dancers and musicians who met to practice improvisation, thinking always in terms of the anti-narrative structural devices of numbers and time (seven people for six minutes, four for four, etc.). A few years later I was lucky enough to open for Mac Low—I was eight months pregnant; he was just a few months from death. The wild beauty of his poems in which meaning was radically unstable, an un-locatable event, while rhythm and sound were activated with the delicate intricacy of wild rose, knocked my own reading right out of my memory. A few years after that, Counterpath Press, the publishing venture I share with my husband, published Mac Low's *154 Forties*, a gathering of 154 poems written at the juncture between centuries and directly inspired by the soundscapes of Hopkins (as Mac Low mentions in his "Note on *154 Forties*"). Here is a portion of the densely sonic and decidedly non-teleological poem, "Forty number 50: Thought Needles," selected for how its title seems specifically to echo Hopkins, as well as for its numbers and flowers:

Wannatalk?   Whadabout?   Montreux   marigolds-
   'n'-ásters
  di-moneta-sáilboat   sunsparks   t'other-shóre
  píne-tree pígeon-roost   foúntain-front   one-two-
    three-four-five-six-báck
  black   dóme   one-two-three-four—tén hazy
    láke   spritzers
    public-flówer-garden fúchia-centered beds   cannas
      afire   statues
  Plénitúde   linkt—curves sassy *Faunésse*[25]

This is poetics built on the plenitude of listening, aimed at, though never arriving at, "pure sound." The diacritical marks, hyphens, and caesuras act as a musical score, directing a performer very specifically in how to vocalize the text (as detailed in Mac Low's "Note"). Mac Low explains that the language has been gathered from words and phrases "seen, heard, and thought of."[26] There is no hierarchy of inner and outer; the language that surrounds us is the language that fills us. When Mac Low wrote these poems in foreign lands, he incorporated the language around him, as you can see here with the use of French and Italian. The editing process, as the gathering process, is sonically driven. "Speech framed to be heard."

Toward the end of his essay on listening, Barthes writes of "free listening . . . a listening which circulates, which permutates, which disaggregates."[27] These verbs can be heard, in a sense, intransitively: free listening permutates the self, disaggregates the self. This is because in the act of free listening, or what we might call Utopian listening, we relinquish our hold on our own narratives, we allow sound to enter us, we "open for" sound. Without transforming it into meanings that we already control, we might allow it to transform us. Barthes speaks of the "risk" involved in listening. To hear a person's desire in his or her voice is to enter into that desire, to become it, "ultimately finding oneself there."[28] Without this risk, which is achieved through the "calm quiet attentiveness" of an "evenly hovering attention," there is a danger of "never finding anything but what is already known" (Freud, quoted in Barthes).[29]

Describing listening to a composition by Mac Low's teacher, collaborator, and friend,John Cage, Barthes writes, "it is each sound one after the next that I listen to, not in its syntagmatic extension, but in its raw and as though vertical *signifying*: by deconstructing itself, listening is externalized, it compels the subject to renounce his 'inwardness.'"[30]

To tank thought is not simply to seek irrationality. It is instead a method of self-renunciation, or a mode of desire, one that doesn't yet know, and may never know, its desired object. *Think Tank*, then: a love poem with no object, an imperfect giving over to the other of sound.

But open ears, o
pen mission (thread, hour, verb)

A sexual strain in the world we
make

plays, bows

its strings[31]

Notes

1. Salome Voegelin, *Listening to Noise and Silence: Towards a Philosophy of Sound Art* (New York: Bloomsbury, 2010), xii.

2. Susan Stewart, *Poetry and the Fate of the Senses* (Chicago: University of Chicago Press, 2002), 101.

3. Jean-Luc Nancy, *Listening*, trans. Charlotte Mandell (New York: Fordham University Press, 2007), 2.

4. Roland Barthes, "Listening," in *The Responsibility of Forms: Critical Essays on Music, Art, and Representation*, trans. Richard Howard (Berkeley: University of California Press, 1991), 245–60.

5. Susan Howe, *Souls of the Labadie Tract* (New York: New Directions, 2007), 17.

6. Voegelin, *Listening*, xiv.

7. Stewart, *Poetry*, 101.

8. Jenny Erpenbeck, *The End of Days*, trans. Susan Bernofsky (New York: New Directions, 2014), 236.

9. Michael Bull, "Auditory," in *Sensorium: Embodied Experience, Technology, and Contemporary Art*, ed. Caroline A. Jones (Cambridge, MA: MIT Press, 2006), 112.

10. Julie Carr, *Think Tank* (New York: Solid Objects, 2015), 6.

11. Voegelin, *Listening*, 3.

12. Barthes, "Listening," 250.

13. In a question and answer period at the University of Naropa's Summer Writing Program in July 2016, just months before her death, Oliveros spoke of the importance not only of hearing and understanding speech but also of learning to listen to the *sounds* of speech. She spoke of "deep listening" as a form of peace and of "tuning out" as a kind of violence enacted at the level of communication.

14. Barthes, "Listening," 253.

15. Stewart, *Poetry*, 79.

16. Walter Benjamin, "The Task of the Translator," in *Illuminations*, trans. Harry Zohn (New York: Schocken Books, 1968), 79–80.

17. Susan Handelman, *Fragments of Redemption: Jewish Thought and Literary Theory in Benjamin, Scholem, and Levinas* (Bloomington: Indiana University Press, 1991), 85.

18. Walter Benjamin, "The Dismemberment of Language," in *The Work of Art in the Age of Its Technological Reproducibility, and Other Writings on Media* (Cambridge, MA: Belknap Press, 2008), 187, 189.

19. Benjamin, "Task," 69.

20. Howe, *Souls*, 18.

21. Carr, *Think Tank*, 7, 10, 12.

22. Gerard Manley Hopkins, *The Journals and Papers of Gerard Manley Hopkins* (Oxford: Oxford University Press, 1959), 289.

23. <u>Spelt from Sybil's Leaves</u>

> Earnest, earthless, equal, attuneable, ' vaulty, voluminous, . . . stupendous
> Evening strains to be time's vást, ' womb-of-all, home-of-all, hearse-of-all night.
> Her fond yellow hornlight wound to the west, ' her wild hollow hoarlight hung to the height
> Waste; her earliest stars, earl-stars, ' stárs principal, overbend us,
> Fíre-féaturing heaven. For earth ' her being as unbound, her dapple is at an end, as-
> tray or aswarm, all throughther, in throngs; ' self ín self steepèd and páshed—quite
> Disremembering, dísmémbering, ' áll now. Heart, you round me right
> With: Óur évening is over us; óur night ' whélms, whélms, ánd will end us.
> Only the beak-leaved boughs dragonish ' damask the tool-smooth bleak light; black,
> Ever so black on it. Óur tale, O óur oracle! ' Lét life, wáned, ah lét life wind
> Off hér once skéined stained véined varíety ' upon áll on twó spools; párt, pen, páck
> Now her áll in twó flocks, twó folds—black, white; ' right, wrong; reckon but, reck but, mind
> But thése two; wáre of a wórld where bút these ' twó tell, each off the óther; of a rack
> Where, selfwrung, selfstrung, sheathe- and shelterless, ' thóughts agaínst thoughts ín groans grínd.

24. As quoted and translated by Andrew Joron, "Accident Over N: Lines of Flight in the Philosophical Notebooks of Novalis," in *Active Romanticism: The Radical Impulse in Nineteenth-Century and Contemporary\ Poetic Practice*, eds. Julie Carr and Jeffrey Robinson (Tuscaloosa: University of Alabama Press, 2015), 245.

25. Jackson Mac Low, *154 Forties*, ed. Anne Tardos (Denver, CO: Counterpath Press, 2012), 101.

26. Ibid., xiii.

27. Barthes, "Listening," 259.

28. Ibid., 256.

29. Ibid., 252–53.

30. Ibid., 259.

31. Carr, *Think Tank*, 77.

The Poet Scholar

As I am a poet-scholar, or, a person who reads and a person who writes, a person who researches and a person who invents—a person who teaches and a person who edits—I can only consider the question of the poet-scholar from the inside—and so what follows is a subjective and gendered account of the position of the poet-scholar in the form of a list 1–10.

1. I entered the academy in order to try to become a better poet. I never saw the two activities—scholarship and poetry—as divided. Though I also thought of writing as belonging to the street, the kitchen, the church, the performance space, the hallway, the subway, the bar, I never imagined that by entering the academy, by becoming a scholar in whatever minor way I could, I would be moving away from poetry. Instead, into it by both direct and circumventive means.

2. In our culture at this time, a scholar (a lucky one) generally has a place, a home, a position, a job, an acknowledged societal role. A poet has none of these things and must either forego them or find them through other activities. I was a mother. And I needed a job. Or there were these children, and they needed a mother. Or, I took a job, one might say, in order to address the situation in which "a woman seek[s] a writerly life in a society still concerned with guarding and protecting the gendering of literary production" (Lisa Robertson).[1] Or I became a scholar because I was a poet and pregnant.

3. I was pregnant in the library, falling asleep with my face on the table.

4. The poet-scholar makes her materials, her sources, evident

in her poems. She also, in her scholarship, announces her pleasures (pleasures in language) out loud. In this way, she places an emphasis on her own body as a material object to be considered, as a source of pleasure to be considered, if not by others (for who knows?) then by her self.

5. The poet might "play," but her vector aims toward grief. To acknowledge, justify, and make available the essential experience of grieving in and through and perhaps for language. The scholar might "work," but her vector aims toward joy. To acknowledge, justify, and make available the essential experience of joy in and through and of language and knowledge, the language of knowledge.

6. And yet the job of the poet is pleasure. The job of the scholar is pain. We could say we bring these two beings together in one body, thus neutralizing or balancing them.

7. The poem constructed of research situates the poet in a library—out of the bedroom, the field, the kitchen, the office, and into the library where she finds materials in order to transforms them. We could call this the "integration of power as an interiorized constraint."[2]

8. I fell asleep in the library to the ongoing autobiography of the male body, a chronology of labor, sex, violence, and accident. I took this archive as a truth and I took it as a fiction.

9. If I am a poet-scholar this means I can renovate my kitchen. I can "meet the Dean"; I can carry a gun to class. I can lock my office door. This means I can shit in the faculty bathroom. I can name the Shakespearian heroines. I can chair the Salary Committee. I can listen to boys and girls as they cry on Adderall. I can order a laptop to be delivered. I can consider King Solomon and Markolf the Fool. I can read French but not German. I can drink at night.

10. If I am a poet-scholar, this means I read the archive. I read the archive and then I make an archive of daily activities and moods. Or I make an archive of the letter T, made to stand for "tree, telephone, tensile, trail and trial." I read an archive of the male body, and then I write an archive of breasts: the old breasts of women in a pool, the new breasts of dancing girls. I read the archive of shooting deaths and

labor theory, and I write an archive of imagined installations and letters to women I've envied. I read the archive of male desire, and I write an archive of my mother's mouth. I entered "the academy" pregnant.

Notes

1. Lisa Robertson, *Nilling* (Toronto: BookThug, 2012), 30.
2. Ibid., 32 (altered).

I Believe That We Will Win

So, the conference happens. It sometimes seems a bit shameful, a little shameful, to go: a form of selling out that also includes fessing up to departmental cash while admitting to your desire, which might be worse than everyone's desire, for attention, but might be more kindly described, by you to yourself, as only the human longing for company. But I did go and those mixed feelings, which also include feeling obliged to represent: the press, the other press, the program, the other program, one's friends, one's fanboy or fangirl desires and crushes, one's "self," got mixed up even more with other things. The visits to the senator's offices, which included a melting-down staffer, staffer to Republican Cory Gardner of Colorado, now of the Trump team, now growing famous for slipping out the backdoor into a waiting car while his protestors/constituents, whom he pretends are paid and eighteen of whom he has arrested, shouted for their own health and dignity. "Meltdown" might be a little wished for, but she did, after dutifully taking notes, and perhaps dutifully calling the group of citizens describing their illnesses and the illnesses of their beloveds "hostile," suddenly gasp and say, "But I voted for Hillary! I'm scared too! No one knows what to do! You have no idea how awful the climate is here!" So that some in our group pitied her and a little bit mothered her, and certainly we apologized for being "hostile," though in fact we knew and loved people who without the ACA would no doubt now be dead or homeless if they were not, in fact, already homeless. And after this meeting we were met by the wind, which blew pretty hard all three days long, but finally calmed at the end of Saturday when I wandered down to the caged and lit White House to join up with everyone, to vigil (stay awake) for our right to speak, but found myself first folding into another group marching and chanting for immigrant rights.

I had the wrong sign, but I got right in step. "Education not Deportation!" and then we made a circle and soon we were yelling, "I Believe That We Will Win! I Believe That We Will Win!" and jumping up and down, all eight hundred of us, jumping up and down to the beat of the chant like children, and joyous, and I started to cry.

But before that there was different crying, in the room with the thousand pointless chairs, where Kazim Ali, Tracie Morris, and I led some writers, who included my sister, an environmental lawyer who works for the DOJ, whose job under Sessions and after cuts will be precarious at best, through a series of breathings and movings and imaginings, all of which had to have been the simplest of beginnings, the most obvious of necessary thinking with our bodies, and I noticed that it had taken so very little to encourage the tears of at least five people, crying because someone had said breathe. And after that there was a moment when I met Jive Poetic, who, to put it briefly, is an Insurgent Poet, creating with others events that are actions and gatherings for learning, such as coat collections (he told me) and voter registrations that are also poetry readings. When I'd asked whether the Insurgent Poets was a closed or an open group, he said, "When you're trying to start an avalanche you don't audition snowflakes," and we laughed so hard about that, twice.

Then later still on the subway after our rally/vigil/march, I was on the train, tired, reading, with my little cardboard sign that said "Prez: Read a Book" leaning on my shin, and a guy across the car said, "James Baldwin," and I said right. It was my mother's copy of *Another Country*, which I had no business bringing to D.C., as the pages were ripping, the back cover having fallen off, and I wanted to preserve her notes, though I couldn't read them.

It was the Dell edition from 1962, having been purchased before my birth for $5.95. She read it, no doubt, in the years she was an organizer of the antiwar and civil rights movements in Cambridge, activities I was born into, carried or strolled into, such that these rallies and marches fill my early memories, vaguely, like extravagant dances I've only half dreamed of.[1] Across the

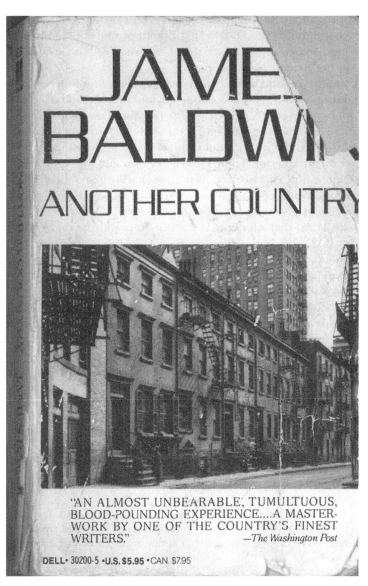

Fig. 1.

advertisement for Dell Books that makes up the book's final page ("Special Offer Buy a Dell Book For Only 50¢") she has written something in black ink. I can read only this: "Once" "Mother" "tree" "black people."

Soon, or immediately, my co-passenger and I are deep in it: Baldwin in Paris, and why did he go, and what it had meant for my co-passenger to have read *The Fire Next Time* as a teenager and his brother, too, who had been in the military and who, having traveled the world, would always say there is nowhere more racist than America. Then we leaned closer and with even more urgency, how can we have a president who hasn't read Baldwin or anyone else, who cannot read or write, whose policies and language seek to entrap, disable, deport, disinform, and destruct, so that suddenly it was our stop and the doors were almost closing, and we bolted and made it out, first him and then me. I stood still for a moment, unsure whether in fact this was my stop, or if instead I'd just leaped because he had and I wanted somehow to stay with him.

I flew home the next morning through an alarmingly bumpy sky with the gift of *Bomb* magazine sticking out of my bag, and there I read the incredible poems of Frances Richard,[2] one that speaks of the Nigerian girls, saying only "girls" in such a way that we know which girls, but as if they are all girls, and her care, Frances's, makes a space for the broken heart to break more. I will end with her question: "how / to notate distance, terror" and only answer that she does, because writing—because books—*are* the social project.

Notes

1. My mother's sardonic critique of violence along with her faith in the power of literature appear here, in a poem she wrote about the deck of a ship on which she and her family traveled to Japan when she was ten:

Oh B-4-C is the place for me
With all the noise plus children's toys
With the yells and screams from nightmare dreams,

With luggage and bags until the ship sags,
With sagging bunks and cluttered floor,
And constant banging on the door,
Little boys fighting, and mothers writing,
There's no place for me but B-4-C.

2. Frances Richard, "The Whole," *Bomb* 138 (Winter 2017), accessed
May 24, 2017, http://bombmagazine.org/article/587215/two-poems.

Another Note on Violence

1. A Spelling Test

daughter
weaver
happiest
celebration
preparation
pleasure
hysterically
piercing
descended
exitement
acknowledge

One error.

What is there to say about the relationships among the words in this fourth-grade spelling test? At first glance, each word seems excited (exited?) to stand alone with none of the others pressing it into service—just an arrangement of letters to be somehow cast into memory.

Then, as is often the way with words, a narrative begins to assert itself: the happiest daughter is the daughter of a weaver, prepared for pleasure and for celebration. At times hysterical, her pleasures are over the top; a kind of unregulated intensity might involve bleeding from an orifice or raving on the floor. "Piercing" could suggest the sharp intelligence of this happiest of daughters, but in its proximity to "hysterically," it invokes violence. Webster's first definition of "to pierce" is "to run through or stab with a weapon." Its second: "to enter or thrust into painfully." This way the verb attaches itself to less happy thoughts, to the one who might threaten her, who might "descend" to thrust, or stab. By list's end I find myself considering the violence within these words. It seems any group of words, in its narrative-generating propensity, delivers a dose of anxiety.

And in fact I can read this spelling test (yanked out of my daughter's backpack) as summarizing the concerns of the book I published in 2010, *100 Notes on Violence*: family (especially mothers and daughters), preparedness, excitement, force, acknowledgment—most of all, acknowledgment. From now on, said someone over drinks, you'll have to be the expert on violence. I am not an expert on violence. What I wanted in writing this book was not to arrive at expertise but to arrive at acknowledgment. Acknowledgement roots in the Old English word *acknow*, which means, among other things, "to confess." In acknowledging violence, I confess to violence—to my own role as participant (as all members of a violent society are violent), or as "witness," but not an innocent one, for in standing by, I acquiesce, I contribute, to suffering.

But acknowledgment and confession are not the only goals of writing. If they were, writing would be an act of pessimism, or at best a request for absolution. This was also not "documentary poetics." I did not want to report my finding, or report them only. Rather, the writing became an active space, not only a reflection (which suggests passivity) but an act of response.

"There's more room in the blues for responding than there is for calling," says Wynton Marsalis during an interview in which he also speaks of the "undying optimism born of the blues." Why optimism? The blues might be considered optimistic simply for how it produces beauty out of suffering. But more radically, if we think of the world (the suffering world) as the call, and the song/poem as a response, then Marsalis hints at a way in which the blues is truly generative. Rather than merely offering a reflection of sorrow, the blues (and poetry when a form of the blues) exceeds the world's call—surpasses suffering by way of invention.[1]

2. I've Nothing Else

"Words rally to the blanks between them," writes Rosmarie Waldrop.[2]

Another way to say this: words in a poem are directed toward nothing, toward no thing. Mimesis is always a fiction. Language leans toward denotation, but literature is always connotative, pressing beyond the immediate sense of words.[3] Writing as a way to *manage* experience creates its own experience. (In this way, the writing of *100 Notes* did not, as many people thought, make me more afraid. It also did not make me less afraid. What it did was give me something to do, something to *make*, while considering fear.)

> 224.
> I've nothing else—to bring, You know—
> So I keep bringing These—
> Just as the Night keeps fetching Stars
> To our familiar eyes—
>
> Maybe, we shouldn't mind them—
> Unless they didn't come—
> Then—maybe, it would puzzle us
> To find our way Home—

Despite her demure opening, Dickinson does not argue that poems (or letters, notes, words) are inadequate, a substitute for the "something else" she does not have. Rather, her poem suggests in its comparisons that just as stars provide the night traveler with her only guide, her only way through or into the night, poems are the one means of "bringing" "nothing" (and nothing else) to the world. And what is nothing? Nothing is possibility (where she dwells, her "Home"); "nothing" is the wild night, the unheard or unseen (the poem/puzzle), the compassless portless Eden of the possible. "Silence is currently what is audible but unintelligible," writes Joan Retallack. "The realm of the unintelligible is the permanent frontier—that which lies outside the scope of the culturally preconceived—just where we need to operate in our invention of new forms of life."[4] Poems serve (up) the future through their effort to represent the no thing. The nothing of Dickinson's Night in this poem stands in opposition to the bright ordinary light of the sun, the "thing" not in the poem.

If poetic language fails to point to a known thing, that's a reason to be afraid of it. But it's also a reason to consider poems as flashes of optimism; invention, which rejects mimesis, moves toward freedom.

Flying across the country: the sky's so clear and we're so low that I get a top-down view of all the cities and towns, all the farms and suburbs, in our path from Denver to New York. Vast stretches of brown farmland (it's November), a river (the Mississippi?) splitting in two. One branch heads to a lake, the other snakes off behind me into something I can't see.

How's everyone doing?
asks the Pilot into silence.

3. Lying

31.

And here I must add the part about the (Wait. Wait longer) Capitol Hill Rapist. We heard about it when we got here from many different people. He'd walk into houses in the middle of the day and rape whomever he found there: men and women, boys and girls.

Only yesterday did someone tell us he stabbed them too. One boy we know, now eight, then five, saw a woman run naked from a house, screaming and bleeding, she died on the street.

His parents said, "She had an ow-y and she fell down."[5]

The boy in this story is a real boy, and what his parents said was also real. Obviously, any child would know that "she had an ow-y and she fell down" was not an accurate way of describing what he saw. The utter failure of the parents to explain the situation speaks about one of the central and anguishing aspects of our culture's love of violence. We do not want our children to know what they know. We do not want to tell them what we have already told them. Protection fails; innocence is false. Something else must be taught to them, which is to say, to us. We continue to live within the paradox of this suffering coupled with experiences of pleasure, hope, even joy. This is not an easy or in any way stable balance. The parents lie to the child in order for him to go on living. He knows they are lying, but perhaps he knows also that they are lying out of love and that love is strangely coexisting with the woman's death: the parents' lie is born of another truth (an over-truth?).

As Oscar Wilde memorably insists, poems, beholden only to their own logic, are always a form of lying. "What is a fine lie?" he asks, "simply that which is its own evidence." Poets, he goes on, "have been really faithful to their high mission [and] are universally recognized as being absolutely unreliable" ("The Decay of Lying").[6] Despite being grounded in a real experience (told to me while the front door stood gaping), despite its ordinary and ordered language, "31" creates a movement *away* from experience. The making of this "other" thing offers up the necessary lie, necessary for how it gives me alternate truths to live by.

> Whereas the floating hand of sexual love stirs the baby's within, the floating arms of Godly love lift the earth to the sun. Whereas trees by the river greening. Girls in the coffee line, ravened and foamed.
>
> *whereas my mouth whereas my vagina. whereas my nipples. whereas my eyes.*[7]

"Whereas" means "in contrast to," "at the same time as," "in view of the fact that." Mouth, vagina, nipples, eyes: these are the permeable spaces through which the world can enter (piercing), through which we create (give life, speak, feed), or through which we perceive the world. The body is vulnerable to penetration and thus to violence, but it's also and therefore capable of expression (in both senses). The little poem "whereas my mouth whereas my vagina" is an equivocal love song to this chiasmus.

Inside any poem, one could say, "nothing breathes, nothing at all"[8] because (and this is something of a relief to me) the poem is a refuge from the living bodies of the children. But there *is* no refuge, no real respite, and so the poem lies and, in lying, makes possible the day.

And the poem, this nothing at all, *does* breathe: Keats's "spirit ditties of no tone," where the word "spirit" reaches back into its Latin root "spirare," meaning "to breathe," suggests at once a silence—a song that is not heard—and a living thing—a nothing that is.

4. Fool

Obscene lilies from the garden droop in a vase too short, their scent vaguely nauseating. In the humid dawn, mosquitoes are out, a few hard dark berries left on the bush.

In a dream my husband and I are hunting deer. On the first day, no luck. On the second, my husband manages to shoot and kill a doe, though neither of us has any idea what to do with the carcass, so we leave it to rot in the woods. On the third day, the animals are on to us. Just as we arrive on the scene, they arrive also, a whole herd of deer and a family of brown bears (as would never happen in real life) there to defend them. We find ourselves running like fools up a wooded hill, rifles hung over our shoulders, banging against our backs.

Finally we make it to town, but not before a child on the road spots us and demonstrates, while laughing, that giving the bears a good slap on their rumps would have been enough to make them run off. In town a mother feeds a baby her bottle. The baby sits in a double stroller, and in the other seat, dressed in a T-shirt, a baby bear. We'd thought these bears dangerous! Evidently not, or not in the way we'd imagined. The bears are wild, but their effect is to tame us—to chase us into town, onto park benches—and to get us to tame them. Does it need to be said that the animals are the children? That this violent dream-story is directed not toward those who might harm us but toward those whom we could easily harm, toward those who force us, by way of their dependency, into civil life?

Judith Butler (responding to Levinas) writes: "Is there something about my apprehension of the Other's precariousness that makes me want to kill the Other? Is it the simple vulnerability of the Other that becomes a murderous temptation for me? If the Other, the Other's face, which after all carries the meaning of this precariousness, at once tempts me with murder and prohibits me from acting upon it, then the face operates to produce a struggle for me, and establishes this struggle at the heart of ethics."[9]

Grapes growing in an arbor here. A blue-green moss on the scrub oak. Soft morning light falls across kitchen knives, a stack of bowls. Depending on which way I turn my attention: happy or furious, depressed or proud, ashamed or righteous, peaceful or agitated, loving or despising, loved or despised. A wasp hovers at the door, heads the other way. I stand up to feed my daughter. All options, all responses, available. Running like fools, trying to outrun the guns banging against our backs.

The word "fool" comes from Latin "follis," which means a leather bag or a bellows. It comes to mean mad or insane or just plain stupid, I guess, because of this image of an empty bag, a bag filled only with air whose only purpose is to blow more air.

According to the ad on my screen, those who look up "fool" in an online etymological dictionary might also be searching for ways to exercise their brains, to avoid dementia. Not only might this person have forgotten the meaning of the word (or any word), she might also be concerned that she has become this, this fool, unable to make sense, prone to dislocation.

> One reason the story
> is discontinuous is that it is,
>
> as each day I wake up neutral
> outside of any story, for awhile
>
> That is so great[10]

writes Alice Notley, speaking of the free space of that "nothing" and sounding here a little like her friend Eileen Myles, who also likes to use the adjective "great" a lot. Myles often says things are "kind of great," inflating and deflating at once.

Like a bellows, like a fool.

In Shakespeare, especially in Lear, the Fool is feminized, a girl-ish man, addicted to unregulated chatter, what Goneril calls "all-licensed" speech. "Ladies too, they will not let me have all fool to myself; they'll be snatching,"[11] says the Fool, possibly hinting at the close connection between himself and that empty space, that nothing, the woman's "snatch" or "purse." And by play's end, the word becomes Lear's term of endearment for Cordelia, the unhappiest daughter, not pierced, but hanged, descending into his arms:

> And my poor fool is hang'd! No, no, no life!
> Why should a dog, a horse, a rat, have life,
> And thou no breath at all? Thou'lt come no more,
> Never, never, never, never, never!
> Pray you, undo this button: thank you, sir.
> Do you see this? Look on her, look, her lips,
> Look there, look there![12]

Lear sees her breathing (deluded fool) because a fool is always full of air, full of potential, the potential of song ("so full of song," says Lear to Fool[13]).

The Fool's own metaphor for the nothing of pure potential, the "no thing" that only he and Cordelia know to value, is an egg with its yolk eaten out, a hollowness that metonymically (if somewhat perversely) resembles that bag in the center of the woman's body, that bag of nothing, the womb.

"Truth's a dog must to kennel, he must be whipped / out," says the Fool early on, whipping out his wit in order to shame (or save) the king.[14] The whip might suggest a phallic counter to this feminized Fool, until I look up that word's etymology as well: whip, from Low German and Middle Dutch *wippen*: swing, leap, dance. The whip is rhyme, is pun and paradox, is the dance of words: the play of poetry.

Today, another form of violence arrives as the candidates propose expansion of oil drilling, a return to coal, the cutting of "discretionary" spending and "entitlements," the end to all unions.

Drought across the heartland while the flames in Texas rise: the effects of a roundabout, long-term, seemingly endless, deeply engrained violence to the earth.

At 1:00 a.m. she wakes crying, and I go in. "The kitty is biting my head and neck!" I settle her back down, "But what about the kitty?" What is violence? A relation between the self and the other? "There is no kitty," I say.

We all know Lear is wrong when he says to Cordelia, "Nothing will come of nothing." But like Lear we fear that nothing will bring us only to more of the same: an emptiness that fails to deliver. And yet, as the play teaches, violence is the result of having no use for nothing. Failing to value the nothing that is, the free space of imagination, the unspeakable silence of love, invites only further losses: "Why should a dog, a horse, a rat, have life, / And thou no breath at all?"[15]

The Fool is a fan of nothing. The poet, a bellowing fool, makes new breath of the nothing that words are:

> Do you see this? Look on her, look, her lips,
> Look there, look there!

Notes

1. In his essay "The Emergency," Andrew Joron writes, "the blues, all blues, are the matrix of the world's subaltern cultures, an expression of triumph in defeat." Later he adds, "contemporary lyricism has been described as the 'singing of the song's impossibility.' This, too, may be a version of the blues—whose strong ontological claim (to manifest the

spontaneous emergence—or emergency—of an unprecedented Cry) now must be renewed." Joron, *Cry,* 5, 10.

2. Rosmarie Waldrop, *Curves to the Apple: The Reproduction of Profiles, Lawn of Excluded Middle, Reluctant Gravities* (New York: New Directions, 2006), 51.

3. Kristeva, *Revolution,* 57–61.

4. Joan Retallack, *The Poethical Wager* (Berkeley: University of California Press, 2003), 345.

5. Julie Carr, *100 Notes on Violence* (Boise, ID: Ahsahta Press, 2010), 32.

6. Oscar Wilde, "The Decay of Lying," *Cogweb,* accessed May 26, 2017, http://cogweb.ucla.edu/Abstracts/Wilde_1889.html.

7. Ibid., 59, 68.

8. Ibid., 76.

9. Butler, *Precarious,* 135.

10. Alice Notley, *Disobedience* (New York: Penguin, 2001), 95.

11. William Shakespeare, *King Lear,* 1608 Quarto, Internet Shakespeare, 1.4:151–52, accessed May 24, 2017, http://internetshakespeare.uvic.ca.

12. Ibid., V.3:283–89.

13. Ibid., I.4:154.

14. Ibid., I.4:211–12.

15. Ibid., IV.3:307–8.

In Defense of Experiences, or,
The Body and the Avant-Garde

I will write as truly as I can from Experience actual indi-
vidual Experience—not from Book-knowledge. But yet it
is wonderful how exactly the Knowledge from good books
coincides with the experience of men. . . . Books are
conversation at present. Evil as well as Good in this, I well
know/ But Good too as well as Evil.
    —S. T. Coleridge[1]

The artists that interest me turn to emotion, feeling, and
affect as a means not of narcissistic escape, but of social
engagement.
    —Jennifer Doyle[2]

What is an avant-garde mandate? What *must* an avant-garde
poem do or not do? Wouldn't such a mandate be immediate-
ly, on release, outdated? In "Poetry on the Brink: Reinventing
the Lyric" (2012), Marjorie Perloff argues that "by definition,
an 'avant-garde mandate' is one that defies the status quo and
hence cannot incorporate it." Logically enough, the only man-
date that would qualify for the front line would be the one that
rejects all other prior or even contemporary practices. A true
avant-garde, it seems, does not look back, or even around. Per-
loff makes her case in opposition to the softer, fence-sitting
claims (she calls them "well-meaning") that she finds in the fol-
lowing passage taken from the introduction to *American Hybrid:
A Norton Anthology of New Poetry*, edited by David St. John and
Cole Swensen:

> Hybrid poems might foreground recognizably experimental
> modes such as illogicality or fragmentation, yet follow the
> strict formal rules of a sonnet or a villanelle. . . . Hybrid po-
> ems often honor *the avant-garde mandate* to renew the forms
> and expand the boundaries of poetry—thereby increasing
> the expressive potential of language itself—while also remain-
> ing committed to the emotional spectra of lived experience.[3]
> (Italics added)

Swensen and St. John say nothing themselves about incorpo-
rating the status quo into this mandate of renewal and expan-
sion, but something in their statements made Perloff think so.
Though they mention the use of received forms, the sonnet and
villanelle, I doubt that Perloff considers such forms status quo,
since hardly anyone uses them anymore and since her essay has
nothing further to say about them. Instead it seems that Perloff
finds the specter of the status quo, something deeply conserva-
tive or even backward, lurking in the language that concludes
Swensen and St. John's statement: "emotional spectra"; "lived
experience."

In his encyclopedic intellectual history, *Songs of Experience:
Modern American and European Variations on a Universal Theme*,
Martin Jay writes that the late twentieth century delivered a
"widespread inclination . . . especially among those who charac-
terized themselves as poststructuralist analysts of discourse and
apparatuses of power, to challenge 'experience' (or the tauto-
logical phrase 'lived experience') as a simplistic ground of im-
mediacy that fails to register the always already mediated nature
of cultural relations and the instability of the subject who is sup-
posedly the bearer of experiences."[4] This critique of experience
shows up often in the high ends of poetry criticism, or shows up
as a general distrust of privileging "the body." To pull, almost
at random, another example from *my* experience, I once asked
conceptual poets Kenneth Goldsmith and Caroline Bergvall to
discuss the tension in their works between the born-digital poem
and live performance, between works that require an interface
and those that require just a face. They were in agreement that
the question did not even merit discussion since there was no
meaningful difference at all between technology and the body

or between physical presence and the mediated experience of being online.[5] Their quick knockdown of the poles I'd set up (probably too simplistically) felt familiar to me as a reader of Romantic and Victorian poetry and criticism, for, in fact, poets and critics have been downplaying the particular value and validity of "lived experience" as an adequate ground for poetry for at least one hundred years, though these earlier poets' ideas of "mediation" were not so much technological as textual.

When in 1853 Matthew Arnold criticized the "Keatsian school" of contemporary poetry, he sneeringly dismissed subjective "expressions" of feeling, calling instead for a return to the poetry of ideas, ideas grounded and sourced from the prior texts of Western culture. The young poet, he argued, "will esteem himself fortunate if he can succeed in banishing from his mind all feelings of contradiction, and irritation, and impatience." Instead he must focus on the "all-important choice of a subject . . . and the subordinate character of expression."[6]

For Arnold, adequate poetic "subjects" were scenes and narratives lifted out of Greek antiquity, the culture he felt most exemplary and most relevant to his own. But the basic argument shares much with Perloff's: art is more valuable and indeed more impactful when it draws from an external source and avoids or codes direct expressions of subjective feeling and personal experience (what Arnold called "the dialogue of the mind with itself").[7] Even if personal feeling is to be your subject matter (as it often is for Susan Howe and Peter Gizzi, two of the poets Perloff writes about in her essay), it'd better be sublimated and mediated by the inclusion of appropriated material. For Arnold this would mean finding in the Greeks a suitable narrative to write through. For a conceptual poet it could mean that with the stroke of a key, personal experience is overlaid, and perhaps overcome, by language from elsewhere. Individual feeling, individual experience, is thus contained within the frame of the dominating and surrounding culture.

A couple of decades before Arnold staked his claim for what we could call an appropriative poetics of ideas, the poet and critic Arthur Hallam remarked on "two kinds of poets"—the "poets of sensation" and the "poets of reflection." For Hallam it's the *former* group that will press readers into a more demanding reading activity, while the latter group will simply "pile [their] thoughts in a rhetorical battery, that they may convince, instead of letting them flow in a natural course of contemplation, that they may enrapture."[8] A poetry of ideas, a fundamentally *conceptual* poetry, asks much less of its readers, argues Hallam, because it addresses them *only* through the intellect. Such idea-driven work, says Hallam, allows the reader to indulge his desire to peruse his author only in a "luxurious passiveness." Hallam's "poet of sensation," in contrast, lives, and so writes, from his embodied emotions, what in today's parlance we call "affect": "for the most important and extensive portion of [the poet's] life consist[s] in those emotions which are immediately conversant with the sensations." "Art is a lofty tree," writes Hallam, "but its roots are in daily life and experience."[9]

The work of the poets Perloff favors in her essay is certainly not *void of* experiences (deaths of loved ones, as she notes), nor are they avoiding emotion. However, she favors these poets because when they write about their experiences, they (supposedly) do so with an affect cooled and regulated by the presence of "other people's words"; they write their experiences by first and foremost acknowledging mediation, by acknowledging that adequate or interesting language is found not "within" but "out there," in some *other.* For Perloff, affect is there to be un-said, or said only obliquely. When suffering presents itself in the poems she examines, she deems it "so overwhelming [it] can hardly be processed." It is the "unsayable." Though in fact the poets she highlights sometimes *do* speak rather directly of their pain, for Perloff their work has value not when it represents raw experience but when, showing more restraint, it serves up cooked and recooked culture.

But method is probably not really the point; to call some work appropriative and other work "lyrical" is a critical convenience (while pointing out that all works are on some level both creative and appropriative is probably equally banal). One could as easily write an essay on the lyrical expressivity of Susan Howe or Peter Gizzi, focusing on the way they turn a phrase, or on the images they choose, rather than on how they incorporate found material. The lines of division Perloff sets up are finally not about our original versus unoriginal geniuses. They are, I believe, much more harshly made scars whose origins lie not in artistic practice but in the kinds of experiences that are felt to be worthy of expression.

So let's examine a bit further what Perloff says she doesn't like about the Rita Dove anthology she is reviewing in the essay I've been discussing. Arguing for the value of digitally sourced, appropriative writing, Perloff writes:

> poets of the digital age have chosen to avoid those slender wrists and wisps of hair [Natasha Trethaway], the light that is always "blinding" [Stephen Dunn] and the hands that are "fidgety" and "damp" [Stephen Dunn], those "fingers interlocked under my cheekbones" [Larry Levis] or "my huge breasts oozing mucus" [Sharon Olds], by turning to a practice adopted in the visual arts and in music as long ago as the 1960s—appropriation.

While some might agree that the language Perloff quotes here, taken out of context, is cloying or clichéd, we should look at what these words describe: wrists, hair, hands, eyes, hand, nerves, fingers, sweat, cheekbones, breasts, mucus: in short, the body. Perhaps it's not "lived experience" in the abstract but bodily experience that's the problem. The body—expressive of emotion, messy and unpredictable, above all vulnerable—what's not to dislike?

Indeed it seems fitting that Perloff closes her essay by referencing Craig Dworkin's effort to replace Orpheus with Echo as the new mythic figure for the poet. Instead of needing to "go down" into the underworld of desire, longing, and loss to find poetic material, the poet can now merely (or not so merely) repeat the words she hears. But what Dworkin does not mention in the introduction to *Against Expression: An Anthology of Conceptual Writing,* where he makes his case for the poetics of Echo, is that when punished by Hera, Echo not only loses her ability to generate original language but eventually loses her body as well. She is the ultimate anorexic girl, invisible in her bedroom, re-tweeting the narcissistic and self-destructive culture back to itself. This is a particularly powerless female image to draw on (but when did our culture ever really like the body of a woman?).[10]

What then might an embodied poetics of experience look like now? What *is* bodily experience in a technologically mediated culture? And what is bodily experience in a society where class, racial, and gendered conflict marks our bodies with such differing levels of vulnerability, suffering, or ease? What might another's bodily experience offer to teach us about our own?

These are the questions I want to bring to my reading. But here I'll turn to an even more fundamental one: what is the body and how *do* we experience it? For it's not only a source of suffering and pleasure, not only a weight that we carry around, are forced to obey or seek to control. It's also inchoate, far more obscured and indecipherable than the code that delivers text and image to our screens. For the body in motion, as all living bodies always are, is not only a location, it is also an action. As Brian Massumi has written in *Parables for the Virtual*, "The charge of indeterminacy carried by a body is inseparable from it (to the extent that it is dynamic and alive) . . . Far from regaining a concreteness, to think the body in movement means accepting the paradox that there is an incorporeal dimension *of the body*."[11]

In a brief essay titled "Utopian Body" from 1966, Foucault remarks on how Utopian fantasies tend to feature an erased body, or a body freed of its mortal flaws (those oozing breasts and sweaty palms). The "great myth of the soul," he writes, is "the most obstinate, the most powerful of . . . utopias with which we erase the sad topology of the body."[12] And yet, Foucault goes on, the body is not so easily reduced. It too has its invisibility, its mysteries, its phantasmagoric qualities:

> [I]t is transparent; it is imponderable. Nothing is less *thing* than my body: it runs, it acts, it lives, it desires, it lets itself be traversed, with no resistance, by all my intentions. . . . Really there is no need for magic, for enchantment. There's no need for a soul . . . for me to be both transparent and opaque, visible and invisible, life and thing. For me to be a utopia, it is enough that I be a body.[13]

The body, the thing we might at times want to escape, is also the "elsewhere" we want to escape to. Not because it houses delight, though it can, but because it is so finally unknowable. Fearing it, disdaining it, sneering at it, we fear, disdain, and sneer at the site of our strangeness to ourselves, the site of our radical belonging to that which is other.

And yet, there is no body; there are only specific bodies. To write from bodily experience is therefore always to write the idiosyncratic details of a life. That such details are hard to get down in all their specificity might be the best reason to try to do it. For it's affect itself that best reveals the fissures running through the social and political structures we participate in. "The body," writes Judith Butler, "implies mortality, vulnerability, agency: the skin and the flesh expose us to the gaze of others, but also to touch, and to violence, and bodies put as at risk of becoming the agency and instrument of all these as well. . . . The body has its invariably public dimension. Constituted as a social phenomenon in the public sphere, my body is and is not mine."[14] This public phenomenon of the body, or of *a* body in particular, is always felt most sharply by those marked by difference, of race and gender and ability most acutely, by those whose "difference" is always in some sense on display.[15] The feeling of being observed, noted, counted, assessed, surveiled, and, in some cases, attacked is a situation of alienated and endangered rootedness that can only be describe from inside it.

It's precisely this tension, then—between the "real life" of the solid and socialized body, which none can get outside of, and the fact that our bodies are never really still, never really knowable, belonging not to ourselves alone but also to the others who surround us, name us, love us or hate us—that poetry can so deeply explore. The writing I find most compelling records, in one way or another, this very tension between what is "self" and what is "other," found so often at the level of sensation.

Such tension might have been ultimately what Perloff hoped to show us in the works of Dworkin, Howe, or Gizzi. But in praising the work that explores such cruxes (and I think their poems do), must one re-inscribe familiar alignments of avant-gardism with anti-authentic, anti-subjective, and anti-corporeal poetry? Might we instead find a different way of understanding the "new," one that doesn't reject body and affect as sources of power and knowledge, even revolutionary power, perhaps as *the* sources of such power? For if poetry is going to have any goals *beyond* bland or ironic repetitions of the status quo, in other words, if it's going to in some way imagine "a world in which things would be different," this world must include the body itself: a site not only of failure and suffering, disgust, and death but also of pleasure, birth, desire, play, intimacy, ambition, and finally, mystery. The body is a marker of difference and the suffering that difference can produce; the body is a marker of presence and the pleasures that presence makes possible; and the body is also the site of our estrangement from even ourselves.

To write "from experience" or "from the body" is not to assume that such terms constitute naïve fantasies of purity or authenticity or naïve faith in the individual as somehow inoculated against cultural bombardments. "Experience," writes art critic Jennifer Doyle, "is not an unquestioned zone of personal truth to which one retreats but a site of becoming, of subject formation."[16] I write not to "reveal myself" (as if I know what's there to be revealed) but to discover what a self might be or be becoming—not in order to turn from the notion of an inner life of sensation but in order to bring to light its inter-action and inter-reliance with all that is "outside."

Notes

1. S. T. Coleridge, *Notebooks: A Selection,* ed. Seamus Perry (Oxford: Oxford University Press, 2002), 86.

2. Jennifer Doyle, *Hold It Against Me: Difficulty and Emotion in Contemporary Art* (Durham, NC: Duke University Press, 2013), xi.

3. Quoted in Marjorie Perloff, "Poetry on the Brink: Reinventing the Lyric," *Boston Review,* May 18, 2012, accessed May 24, 2017, http://www.bostonreview.net/forum/poetry-brink.

4. Martin Jay, *Songs of Experience: Modern American and European Variations on a Universal Theme* (Berkeley: University of California Press, 2006), 2.

5. Based on performances I've seen Bergvall do since then, I would guess that she no longer holds this position, if she even fully held it then. And of course Kenny Goldsmith's *Fidget* reveals his fascination with the body, just as his Soliloquy reveals his fascination with the self and its expressions.

6. Matthew Arnold, "Preface of 1853," *Bartleby.com,* accessed May 24, 2017, http://www.bartleby.com/254/1002.html.

7. Ibid.

8. Arthur Hallam, "On Some of the Characteristics of Modern Poetry, and on the Lyrical Poems of Alfred Tennyson," 3, accessed May 24, 2017, http://www.uwyo.edu/numimage/texts/hallam%201831.pdf.

9. Ibid., 4,5.

10. A fourteen-line poem on the female body

1. It has to begin somewhere
2. She harass with enjoyment
3. Tired of the topic before I
4. Start. Cause if she's not raped
5. She's the criminal killing the
6. Thing. So rape her to
7. Save her from herself. O
8. Lovely
9. Flakey, she'll be data or she'll be tagged
10. So she made herself a border and hung there
11. Pregnant or bleeding or pregnant and bleeding
12. Been full a long time with
13. Time and the grey clouds streaming in
14. We're not always dead

11. Brian Massumi, *Parables for the Virtual: Movement, Affect, Sensation* (Durham, NC: Duke University Press, 2002), 5.

12. Michel Foucault, "Utopian Body," in *Sensorium: Embodied Experience, Technology, and Contemporary Art,* ed. Caroline A. Jones (Cambridge, MA: MIT Press, 2006), 230.

13. Ibid., 231.

14. Butler, *Precarious,* 26.

15. Though some of the lines of poetry Perloff quotes as negative examples are written by white writers, it seems not circumstantial that the volume under attack was edited by a black woman, for race is at issue throughout Perloff's essay. Perloff makes clear that underneath her fight with "folksy" poems is a deeper critique of certain so-called ethnic (nonwhite) poetry when, in her opening narrative, she describes how the intellectual rigor of the Language Poets became muddled when questions of "identity" forced their hand. Her prime example of a bad and too "folksy" poem is one by black poet Natasha Tretheway that features bodily pain. As Ken Chen, discussing Kenny Goldsmith's infamous performance "The Body of Michael Brown," writes, "Conceptual

Poetry could not ethically grapple with the murder of Michael Brown, since its mission has been to disappear the racial body. Seeing themselves as post-body, post-racial, and post-identity, the Conceptual Poets view identity as either redacted and irrelevant or fluid and mutable, a signifier ping pong that, after information technology and global capitalism, never stops or stands still." Ken Chen, "Authenticity Obsession, or Conceptualism as Minstrel Show," *Asian American Writers' Workshop,* July 31, 2016, accessed May 24, 2017, http://aaww.org/authenticity-obsession.

16. Doyle, *Hold It Against Me,* 146.

No Video: On Anne Carson

Invited to write an essay on Anne Carson's work, I balked.

I first read Carson when I was twenty-three: *Glass Irony and God* had just been published. I read "The Glass Essay" and gave up. Gave up what? Gave up not loving is what I want to write. That is very dramatic and in no way true. But so is "The Glass Essay" very dramatic and possibly not true. Carson's "I" sat on her living room floor conjuring images, "naked glimpses of [her] soul." I was a dancer—I knew something about the images the mind can make, since despite its athletics, a lot of dancing happens in the mind. We danced with and in the mind's hallucinatory blasts. My mother was having back problems. I told her to lie on the floor and think of her back spreading out like pancake batter in the pan. She'd been making us pancakes for two decades. But pancakes were not just "comfort food," they were a defining symbol of my affiliation—my affiliation with the female side. My mother used to say that my parents' divorce was, finally, on account of pancakes. Not feminism, not affairs, but a fundamental difference about pancakes. He made them thick, with yogurt mixed in. She made them thin, more like crepes. They didn't like each other's, and I liked hers. I was loyal, for I lived with her. Despite her episodic rage, despite various hard slaps and one or two sharp kicks to my shin, I was loyal to her, to her love and also to her pancakes. Therefore, when I said, "Imagine your back spreading out like pancake batter in the pan," I was offering more than a dancer's image. I was offering a sign of my loyalty, my affiliation with the female. My father's pancake batter did not spread out on the pan. It sat there, more or less stiff, and browned.

I read "The Glass Essay" for the first time and encountered

Carson's "I," facing her mother across a kitchen table or sitting on her living room floor, bereft of her lover, "Law," conjuring images. (Ladislaw from *Middlemarch* was my literary crush at that time. His curly head, his lad-like vague artistic ambitions, attracted me like no other. But understand, it was not that I wanted him; I wanted to *be* him—*Ladislaw*, the lad that *is*, that must be, that gets to be, the bearer of the law. Not Dorothea Brooke with her prim morality, and certainly not her floosy sister. Like Mary-Anne Evans herself, I wanted to be the boy, the lad, the George, aloof and unperturbed, to "live in my lantern / Trimming subliminal flicker / Virginal."[1] "It's better to be a neuter," wrote Carson.[2]) I found "Anne" in the midst of what she called her "spiritual melodrama," and I thought I knew what she was up to. I'd conjured images, too, though in the studio, that land of fantastic terror and delight.

"When Law left I felt so bad I thought I would die. / This is not uncommon," I read, tasting that curious blend of pathos and sardonicism that marks so much of Carson's work. So, I could sweat and shrug at once. Good. I kept going, into *Eros* (1998), into *Men* (2000).

Much of "The Glass Essay" is concerned with memory—a problem for those who remember, much worse for those who do not. "Perhaps the hardest thing about losing a lover," she writes, "is / to watch the year repeat its days."

> I can feel that other day running underneath this one
> like an old videotape.[3]

It's a poison, this "other day," this previous April 11, this video under real life. Memory is pain, whether happy or sad. In "The Glass Essay," Carson's father has Alzheimer's disease. She describes becoming aware that he no longer knows who she is on the phone, though he tries hard to be friendly. That year my mother had back pain, but a decade later, she would not remember the words to "Itsy-Bitsy Spider" or how to count change. For a while I took pride in the fact that she still knew me, seemed "just fine" when talking on the phone. I bragged about how few words she forgot during our conversations, just as you might brag about how a baby smiles at you. My stepfather, knowing what I was after, said, "That's because speaking to you makes her happy." Maybe her pleasure in me could keep her—not just alive, but "solvent," I want to say "solvent."

Solvent: able to pay one's debts, able to dissolve other substances within one's self. The two meanings seem in some kind of contradiction—the first directs itself outward, the second draws in. A solvent mother would do both at once: give what she owes while offering a within to enter and become. The mother with dementia can do neither.

Memory is bitter and no-memory is sick.

"My robotic nausea" is a phrase that presented itself to me when I found myself pregnant for the seventh time in my twenty-five years of "solvency." This one, like the first, was a pregnancy fit for nothing but the table. "Robotic nausea" is also a good way to describe the sensation that arises on the way up to the fifth floor where my mother resides in a chair. Her hair has been cut with no concern for fashion, but her breath no longer stinks; they brush her teeth here, evidently. The fifth floor's where old women play with dolls if they can and old men announce themselves prepared for lunch all day long. Memory is bitter and no-memory is robotic nausea.

Carson has been milling the bitterness of memory since I was twenty and probably much longer than that. I know almost nothing about her, but I know her mother died in 1997, no longer carefully chewing lettuce at the kitchen table while asking questions about the airport. No longer dangling her feet in some Canadian pond. Carson compares death to a crossed out sentence, there and not there at once, like that video running under every calendar day. "To my mother, / love / of my life, I describe what I had for brunch," she writes some years after her mother is gone.[4]

The scents of oranges and geraniums are my mother's scents. Before her mouth began to stink, she passed peeled oranges from the front seat to the back. Geraniums bloomed year-round in a yellow kitchen. That day running under this one. Bitter scent of orange and dirt.

Invited to write about Anne Carson's work, I balked. There was no way not to emulate. And no way not to be sentimental. For though I would never write, as she wrote, "I am not a sentimental person," I am easily embarrassed, also easily *embarazada* (pregnant). What these two tendencies have to do with one another, I cannot say, but to broaden it, perhaps I am not very protected. "Solvent" comes from the Latin verb "solvere," which means "to loosen, to unfasten." "Contact is crisis," she wrote ("Dirt and Desire"[5]), a phrase I took as an epigraph for my first book. And so, concerned about my tendency to gush, I thought instead of writing about her writing, I'd write about the dances.

I'd seen "Bracko" and "Nox," her collaborations with dancer-choreographer Rashaun Mitchell, at the Institute for Contemporary Art in Boston in the summer of 2011. My father and stepmother bought the tickets, but they didn't love the show. To them, and they didn't say this, but I knew, Carson was too cold, too distant, too intellectual in her delivery of the text. The contrast between her Canadian chill, her academic correctness, and, in "Nox," Mitchell and fellow dancer Silas Riener's wild boyish abandon made little sense to them, or at least did not move them. For me it was different. Carson didn't have to be in any way "passionate." She didn't even have to be good. It was better, in fact, that she was somewhat tight, awkward, not really a performer, but a little like someone in my department arguing for curriculum revisions. This way I could watch her un-intruded, in a kind of privacy. Everyone loved the boys: they dashed around, did sexy impossible moves, breathed hard, and really meant it! But I kept one eye on awkward Anne, pushing around her little podium on wheels, reading from her book. One likes, in admiring, a certain seclusion. It's better, as John Donne knew, if the world does not participate. (The world, actually, does participate in admiring Anne Carson, but my parents were enough world for me—their quiet response was enough to amplify my enthusiasm.)

And so I thought I'd write about the dance. But in order

to do that well (I'd taken a dance criticism class with Jennifer Dunning in college!), I needed a video, or I needed to see the dances again so I could at least take notes. I wrote to Anne. "We have no video and we are not doing it again," she wrote back, and then, "Good luck."

This was not all she wrote, but it was all that I remembered.

As she tells it, her father's teeth grew black in the nursing home.

Of course I do not know if I read Anne Carson first when I was twenty-three or twenty-eight, or some age between. The floor I see her sitting on, conjuring her visions, is the living room floor of my Brooklyn Heights apartment where I lived between the ages of thirty and thirty-four. But that means nothing, says nothing about truth. In that apartment I became pregnant four times. In those years, my mother was still OK, though her mother died in March of the final year I lived there. At the funeral—a meager chilly affair, just the family and Rabbi Millner clutching our jackets in the tiny Maine graveyard, the little kids, Nina and Benjamin, running around the graves—my mother, having very little nice to say about her own mother, decided instead to list all her descendants. This would be a way to honor her as the matriarch whose blood we shared. But my mother could not remember everyone's name. Worst of all, she forgot my brother's wife and daughter entirely, though they were standing (or playing) right there. Later, she was mortified and apologized profusely. But this was not simply grief or the late winter cold numbing her mind: this was the beginning of her dementia, and we all knew it.

Memory fails. Or freezes: I had my own terrible secret that weekend and "I wish I could forget" (Apollinaire, "Zone"). Asked if we wanted to say or read something at the gathering, none of us did. Memories of my grandmother: one gift of a talking doll ("dance-with-me" *robotic nausea*), her panicked calls to my mother, one, then another, abusive husband, her underwear on the outside of her pants: Bitter gist, here we go.

Who can sleep when she—
hundreds of miles away I feel that vast
    breath
fan her restless decks.
Cicatrice by cicatrice
all the links
rattle once.
Here we go mother on the shipless
    ocean.
Pity us, pity the ocean, here we go.
                        — "Sleep Chains"[6]

The video-less dance exists, then, as the following: A history, which, as Carson tells us in the opening pages of *Nox*, is always akin to elegy: "The word 'history' comes from an ancient Greek verb ἐπερωτάω meaning 'to ask.' . . . But the asking is not idle. It is when you ask about something that you realize you yourself have survived it, and so you must carry it, or fashion it into a thing that carries itself."[7]

And so: The wildest boy, the "Brother," runs behind the glass wall that forms the back of the stage. Beyond him, Boston Harbor, summer light low. He does not "run," he *tears*. Forward and back, before ample boats. He is, we might think, "lost," but not dead.

The two men, I'll call them "Brother" and "Sister," wrapped in a crazy embrace on the floor. "Brother" is somehow both inside out and upside down in "Sister's" arms and legs. She holds him, or she *autopsies* him: "Autopsy is . . . a mode of authorial power. . . . I wonder what the smell of nothing is. Smell of autopsy."[8]

"Brother" and "Sister" spread themselves against a wall. Walls are useful in dance, for they make of the body a form, not just an activity. They provide a sliding dimension, a surface for slamming. This wall dance is not original. It is slightly amateurish. And this is why I like it and why I (think I) remember it. Here "Brother" and "Sister" are like kids making treasure maps in the linen closet. Not very original, and not necessarily great, but very dear.

After, there is a Q and A in which I do not want to speak to Carson. I prefer to remain an enthusiast, fan, lover, aficionado, admirer; informal buff, bum, freak, nut, fiend, fanatic, addict, maniac. A follower, adherent, supporter, advocate, disciple, votary, member, stalwart, zealot; believer, worshiper. Not one who receives an answer. So I ask the boys things. Which they answer with lies.

Nox is, as most people reading this already know, an accordion book, which is to say, a staircase. Up and down is how you read, or can if you lift it up out of the box, rather than folding it open. A vertical reading is like listening to a deaf person's hands. It requires a new perspective. But "up and down" is one way we've understood the movement of poetry for a very long time. Since Orpheus at least, we imagine the poet traveling "downward" to find material, bringing that material back "up." Blanchot: "Orpheus' work does not consist of securing [the work] by descending into the depths. His *work* is to bring it back into the daylight and in the daylight give it form."[9] One also imagines traveling "down" into memory.

But toward what?

History can be at once concrete and indecipherable. Historian can be a storydog that roams around Asia Minor collecting bits of muteness like burrs in its hide. Note that the word "mute" (from Latin *mutus* and Greek μύειν) is regarded by linguists as an onomatopoeic formation referring not to silence but to a certain fundamental opacity of human being. . . . To put this another way, there is something that facts lack. "Overtakelessness" is a word told me by a philosopher once: *das Unumgangliche*—that which cannot be got round. Cannot be avoided or seen to the back of. And about which one collects facts—it remains beyond them.[10]

Carson speaks these words as the men dance. That their dancing is beautiful is a thing that cannot be said; to say so makes it less true than if one were to remain silent. Why a dancer is beautiful is something I've never understood. After all, I don't find anything particularly beautiful about the "human form." Though oddly, as I recall the "fundamental opacity" of the dance, recall very few "facts," of this history, into me drops the word my mother used to express surprise: "heavens." Heavens.

To read the book is to experience it falling. Lift it up and it falls back down, turn the page and rest it on the table and you risk a tumbling, and the need to re-gather, to pack it away. This awkward reading/spilling is not unlike the effort to remember, the effort to describe two men running, dropping to the ground, catching each other at the back of the head. Who would ever want to be a dance critic? Who would ever want to be a historian?

Better to be a poet—whose failure to catch the uncatchable
    story is a given.

—

The brother lies down. Next to
The ~~book sister mother~~.

—

No video.

Notes

1. Mina Loy, *The Lost Lunar Baedeker* (New York: Farrar, Straus and Giroux, 1997), 225.

2. Anne Carson, "Stanzas, Sexes, Seductions," in *Decreation: Poetry, Essays, Opera* (New York: Vintage, 2006), 72.

3. Carson, *Glass, Irony and God* (New York: New Directions, 1995), 8.

4. Carson, "Lines," in *Decreation*, 5.

5. Carson, *Men in the Off Hours* (New York: Vintage, 2001), 150.

6. Carson, *Decreation*, 3.

7. Carson, *Nox* (New York: New Directions, 2010), 1.1.

8. Ibid., 1.2.

9. Blanchot, *Gaze*, 99.

10. Carson, *Nox*, 1.3.

Muse X

Lyn Hejinian's Oxota:
A Short Russian Novel

Genres are not to be mixed. I will not mix genres.
—Jacques Derrida[1]

Within this injunction/promise /prediction lies a broader de-
mand for order, clarity, and accommodation, for established
norms, rules, and codes, and for obedience. And yet Derrida
will go on to suggest that the "law of genre" always holds within it
its own perversion, its own betrayal: "What if there were, lodged
within the heart of the law itself, a law of impurity or a principle
of contamination?" he writes. "And suppose the condition for
the possibility of the law were the *a priori* of a counter-law, an
axiom of impossibility that would confound its sense, order, and
reason?"[2]

Derrida locates this ever-present transgression in the pro-
pensity of genres to announce themselves, either directly (as in
the subtitle A Short Russian Novel) or indirectly, as when a text
does something genre specific (a poem justifies left or a novel
foreshadows). Such moments of genre performance, argues
Derrida, are the moments when the genre stops *being itself* in
order to *speak about itself.* Just when most stridently announcing
its adherence to the "law," the genre breaks out of its natural or
total adherence to that law and thus creates an opening. "Mak-
ing genre its mark, a text demarcates itself."[3]

This argument feels very particular to its moment; all the sur-
prise attacks of deconstruction might, in 2016, inspire a smile
rather than a gasp. Nonetheless, it resonates quite immediately

with an idea we now hold about gender—that term that always seems so close to genre, and not only because of orthography— an idea that's been part of academic understandings of gender at least since Judith Butler's *Gender Trouble* and part of a (counter)cultural understanding of gender for much longer (for behind *Paris Is Burning*, Cindy Sherman, Riot grrrl, and straight-edge boys in plaid and Carhartt, we had Oscar Wilde's carnations and cloaks, Baudelaire's prostitute performing the "barbaric elegance . . . of her own invention"[4]). "What is called gender identity is a performative accomplishment compelled by social sanction and taboo. In its very character as performative resides the possibility of contesting its reified status," wrote Butler in 1988.[5] In the performative status of genre too (of all genre at all times) lies the possibility of its own transgression. Or, as literary critic Dino Felluga puts it, "the self-conscious remarking of genre within a text not only ensures the interpretation of texts but also ensures the performative instability of generic form."[6]

I'm interested in tracing the interplay between the performance and transgression of genre and the performance and transgression of gender in three texts from three different periods, the Victorian, the Modernist, and the contemporary, and in revealing how all three lean on figures of androgyny as muse, a muse I'll call "Muse X," for the transgressions they seek and perform.

Derrida introduces the theme of "gender" by way of a parenthetical aside early in his essay when he is attempting to broaden the concept of "genre" to mean something like "category." But as we move toward the end of the essay, we see that "gender" has been his true theme all along:

> The question of the literary genre is not a formal one: it covers the motif of the law in general, of generation in the natural and symbolic senses, of birth in the natural and symbolic senses, of the generation of difference, sexual difference between the feminine and masculine genre/gender, of the hymen between the two, of relations between the two, of an identity and difference between the feminine and the masculine.[7]

Reading Blanchot's *La Folie du jour*, Derrida argues that the real thrust of this strange mixed-genre work is not to say something about the permeability of literary genres but rather to say something about the permeability of genders, to make a case for the neutral, trans, or mixed gender of the narrator/protagonist: "'I,' then, can keep alive the chance of being a fe-male or of changing sex."[8] The mixing of genres is an opportunity or metaphor for the blending or mixing of genders. Or as Kazim Ali puts it, "Perhaps the genre-defying writer is a queer one, who understands gender and genre derive from the same classifying, categorizing impulse—the impulse not to invent, but to consume, commodify, *own*."[9] Perhaps Derrida indicates much more broadly that formal experiment makes possible an expansion at this ground floor of social organization.

Let me move back now to the middle of nineteenth-century England where the "law of gender" was particularly strangling to women, where laws around women's ability to own property, hold custody of their children, pursue education or career were beginning to face a long and urgent process of contestation.

Elizabeth Barrett Browning published her "poem-novel" *Aurora Leigh* in 1856 at the beginning of the women-led effort toward marriage reform.[10] Until the Married Women's Property Acts of the 1870s and early 1880s, a married woman, under common law, could not own or will personal property.[11] All that a woman owned prior to marriage was forfeited to her husband; all her subsequent earnings were also legally his. This legal reality was, as many have shown, consistent with an ideology in which a married woman's identity was subsumed into the identity of the husband. As the often-quoted late eighteenth-century saying puts it, "In law husband and wife are one person, and the husband is that person."[12]

Barrett Browning was extremely active in the effort to reform these laws. In fact, the petition for the first Married Women's Property Act (1870) was sometimes referred to as "the petition of Elizabeth Barrett Browning, Anna Jameson, Mary Howitt, Mrs. Gaskell" (the other three women were important activists for feminist causes).[13] While the conclusion of *Aurora Leigh* in some senses offers us a traditional "marriage plot," it presents this plot with full awareness that the denouement of such narratives were problematic for women. As much as the poem can be read as reinforcing Victorian marriage ideology, it must also be read as leveling a serious and sustained critique against the Victorian "law of gender."

For those not familiar: the novel opens with Aurora, a recently orphaned young woman who must leave Italy to live with her paternal aunt in England. She is literary and ambitious, a poet, and yet these qualities are significantly squelched by her strict and conventional aunt who believes women should (as Aurora satirically puts it) "keep quiet by the fire / And never say 'no' when the world says 'ay,'" that they are best put to use to "fatten household sinners."[14]

Aurora meets Romney Leigh, her cousin and the heir to her father's fortune (which will become "hers" too if she marries him). Romney, a young man with socialist leanings, mocks Aurora's poetry, arguing that she cannot in fact write great works because of her gender. Women, argues Romney, cannot really be poets because they tend to focus on the details of life (experience) rather than on broad generalities (abstractions and ideas): "You generalize / Oh, nothing,—not even grief! Your quick-breathed hearts, / So sympathetic to the personal pang / . . . . The human race / To you means, such a child, or such a man, / You saw one morning waiting in the cold."[15]

Here we have a familiar dichotomy and a familiar critique. Women feel too much to be useful to general public concerns. Their strength lies in their attention to particulars, to subjective experiences, to "the dust of the actual."[16] General matters, matters of politics, philosophy, and morals, what Aurora calls "universals," belong only to the male. (But Romney doesn't find Aurora entirely useless. On the contrary, he finds her marriageable. His proposal elicits only scorn from Aurora, who, recognizing his hypocrisy, retorts with great sarcasm "Anything does for a wife."[17]) "Woman as you are," continues Romney,

> Mere woman, personal and passionate,
> You give us doating mothers, and perfect wives,
> Sublime Madonnas, and enduring saints!
> We get no Christ from you—and verily
> We should not get a poet in my mind.[18]

What's behind this slide from Christ to poet? Is it simply that Christ in his martyrdom takes on universal suffering, something that poets are supposedly attuned to? That is, it seems, how Romney sees it.

But Christ was British culture's dominant symbol for the fusion of just the opposing qualities that Romney (and the culture at large) has so deftly gendered. As Murray Krieger writes, "Through the mysteries of Christ's double—and doubly paradoxical—status as man and as God, the worldly body can contain the undying spirit, as worldly history can contain the eschatological or the Old Testament can contain the New."[19] At once human and divine, at once time-bound individual and timeless figure for universal compassion and love, Christ joins these gendered categories in one body. Romney's claim "We get no Christ from you" becomes a challenge for Aurora, for Browning, to discover precisely how we might locate Christ in the body of a woman, or in the body of a woman's text. And though it can be said that Browning produces a Christ figure in the actual body of the martyred character Marian, to me it's the text's form, the genre-blending text itself, that best becomes that androgynous typological transgression.

One of the most often quoted passages in *Aurora Leigh* reveals how Browning imagines just this blending of universal truths and concrete particulars in generic terms.

> The critics say that epics have died out
> With Agamemnon and the goat-nursed gods.
> I'll not believe it, I could never deem
> . . .
> That Homer's heroes measured twelve feet high.
> They were but men:—his Helen's hair turned grey
> And Hectors infant whimpered at a plume
> As yours last Friday at a turkey-cock.
> . . .
>
> But poets should
> Exert a double vision; should have eyes
> To see near things as comprehensively
> As if afar they took their point of sight,

And distant things as intimately deep
As if they touched them. Let us strive for this.[20]

The domestic novel (a feminized form) thus meets the epic poem (gendered male) through the doubled vision of the new poet: she who can see "near things" as deeply as "distant." This "double vision" is, then, Christ's vision, for by virtue of his double ontology, Christ finds intimacy with universal and individual suffering alike.

The marriage plot allows Browning to present two ways of life, two ways of seeing, to mark their differences and then to reunite them only when the domination of one over the other is undone. At their reunion, Romney's been beaten down by disappointments and failure while Aurora has succeeded wildly in her ambitions. Further, Romney's been maimed; he becomes marriageable only after fire has destroyed his sight (here Browning imitates or appropriates the blinding of Rochester in *Jane Eyre*). Only after this blinding is "double vision" possible, for patriarchy's violence demands a violent undoing. And while the marriage of Romney and Aurora is not the making of a mixed or queerly gendered person, while it can't fairly be read as a total rejection of patriarchal ideologies, my point is that the mixed-gendered "person" *is* figured, formally, in the text itself: mixed genre becomes the mixed gender that Browning cannot quite articulate narratively. As it "marries" domestic and localized material with epic form, the text itself achieves the "double vision" of an un- or neutrally gendered Christ.

Let me now turn to a more recent mixed genre text that features more concretely a crucial figure of androgyny: William Carlos Williams's *Paterson*. A debate between genres and their propensities, or between genders and theirs, is offered quite early on in *Paterson* through the figure of Marcia Nardi. But we can look to the opening of Book I to see that Williams is at all times alert to the same tension—between the general/universal and the particular/subjective—as *Aurora Leigh.* "To make a start / out of particulars / And make them general," begins Williams.[21] This is Browning's "double vision" seemingly achieved—the two poles already wed. And yet the marriage between particulars and generalities (or things and ideas) proves a bit rockier than that. Trouble is announced through the inclusion of the difficult, unhappy voice of Marcia Nardi.

Nardi's letters to the doctor ("Paterson" in the text), rendered in prose, complain about the breakdown of their friendship. She feels ignored, tossed aside, disregarded. She's distraught, lonely, and broke. But when their personal relationship is not taking center stage, Nardi describes another point of contention in their differing attitudes toward writing. Nardi accuses the doctor of writing a literature "disconnected from life," one that cares about other people only "theoretically—which doesn't mean a God damned thing."[22]

Nardi advocates instead for literature grounded in what Aurora would call the "dust of the actual," the particulars of real life. Indeed, Williams is concerned with this too—drawing on history, news, personal letters, and other detritus of the real throughout *Paterson*. And yet, in giving Nardi such a dominant position, in highlighting her prose letters rather than her poems (which Williams also had access to), Williams genders genre: poetry, the genre of abstraction and idealization, of general ideas and universal themes, belongs to "Paterson," to the male voice. Prose, the genre of detail, of fact, of messy and subjective material realities, belongs to Nardi, the book's central female.

And yet Williams, like Browning before him, seeks to unite these voices. One could say that *Paterson* is all about that, bringing genders and genres together between the covers of a single volume. But Williams also *figures* this meeting or blending of genres/genders in a body that appears in the middle of Book V (1958), his Muse X:

> There is a woman in our town
> walks rapidly, flat bellied
>
> In worn slacks upon the street
> . . .
>   Neither short
> nor tall, nor old nor young
> her
>   face would attract no

adolescent. Grey eyes looked
straight before her.
      Her
         hair
was gathered simply behind the
ears under a shapeless hat.

Her
   hips were narrow, her
            legs
thin and straight. She stopped

me in my tracks—until I saw
her
   disappear in the crowd.
. . . .
she was dressed in male attire,
as much as to say to hell

with you.
. . .
have you read anything I have written?
It is all for you[23]

This androgynous muse, this woman in male dress who says "to
hell with you" to patriarchy, answers the problem of gender that
is also a problem of genre (or vise versa). She fascinates because
her defiance points forward to the political freedom of women,
and by extension of all people, but also because in her androgy-
nous form she unites not only genders but also the two opposing
efforts of Williams's writing: the first being to touch the actual,
the other being to imagine the possible. That is why she is at
once desirable and distant, at once a real woman with erotic ap-
peal and an ideal muse figure, neither short nor tall, young nor
old: in other words, an abstraction, for whom Williams writes.

There is much more to say about how *Paterson* (and also *Au-
rora Leigh*) works through these desires. In a longer essay I'd
say something about how Williams abandons this androgynous
muse and replaces her with his "son" (Ginsberg). But I'll turn
now to my final text, Lyn Hejinian's *Oxota: A Short Russian Novel*

(1991), in order to see how a writer more recently manages to thematize the blending of genres and genders as a means toward dissolving the damaging oppositions articulated by cousin Romney, these oppositions that continue to exert control over our writings and our identities.

First, I should say the obvious—that from *Aurora Leigh* to *Oxota* the poem-novel has come a very long way. Though Hejinian includes characters, scenes, and events, the links between them are never particularly clear or sustained. As Jacob Edmund has written, "*Oxota*'s sentences do not appear to relate to one another in a linear way. . . . narrative fragments appear everywhere . . . while never taking the form of a coherent whole."[24] Marjorie Perloff reads the book's style as the result of competing aesthetic urges, writing, "But how, we might ask, do we reconcile the poetics of the language movement with the demands of narrative?"[25]

But these stylistic difficulties also reveal, I think, the ways in which Hejinian attempts to disturb the gendered binaries of political history and domestic life, of the general with the particular, and of the ideal with the real. One could say, in fact, that *Oxota*—set in Russia in and around glasnost, but seeming to take place almost entirely within the kitchens and living rooms of friends—realizes, more successfully than *Paterson*, the marriage of the political and the daily, the historical and the intimate. Indeed, Hejinian announces her rejection of the oppositions facing Browning and confronted by Williams at the start of Book 3:

> So I must oppose the opposition of poetry to prose.
> Just as we can only momentarily oppose control to
> discontinuity, sex to organization, disorientation to domestic
>   time and space, and
>   glasnost (information) to the hunt[26]

And earlier:

> The mere mood of our words was producing content
> The sheer detail was required
> Sleep is an orientation
> There's no need to distinguish a poem from prose[27]

Exposing the lie in the structure of genre law, Hejinian refuses to hierarchize Aurora's double vision. The "moods" and "details" so present throughout *Oxota* are not distinct or outside of the capital-H History that frames the book and might be considered its "general" subject matter.

As any reader of this vast and deeply disjunctive text will experience, our expectations around prose and poetry are not so easily dissuaded. No matter what pleasure we might find in passages like this: "Take a naked doll and a spoon, a lifted city / A great pastiche / You're wrong / I was straightening the blanket around where I sat, while Vasya turned up the tape machine," for most of us they will be very different pleasures than the ones we discover in so-called realist novels where events and commentary on such events organize around causalities.

If Hejinian is, then, transgressing genre by refusing to satisfy readers' expectations, how is this tied to a theory of gender? In her 1991 interview "Comments for Manual Brito" Hejinain writes:

> There tends to be some confusion or misconception, inherent maybe to Western thinking, which assumes a separation between, for example, form and content, verb and noun, process and condition, progress and stasis. But in fact these pairs and their parts constitute a dynamic, a momentum, a force. Quantities are change, not categories. . . . By the way, this can be said for gender, too—man and woman. Being a woman isn't a state so much as it's an impetus, with certain momentum, occurring at various velocities and in various directions. . . . Or one could speak about literary form, which isn't form at all but force.[28]

While the oppositions Hejinian lists here (states versus forces) can't be mapped directly onto those we've been discussing (generalities versus particularities), we can see that for Hejinian oppositions or binaries are inherently problematic, perhaps most of all when they become gendered. Gender law, like genre law, provides us only with false choices. We must write as we live, dynamically.

The androgynous figure doesn't play as strong a role in *Oxota* as it does in Hejinian's later work, *A Border Comedy*, where she writes (just one of many examples) of "changing sexes / in changing dreams" where "A breast appeared, off me, but incompletely / On the man I am / A woman / I or she / All of this being 'gender by degrees.'"[29] *Oxota* (like its model, Pushkin's *Eugene Onegin*) is more frequently concerned with loosening the boundaries between art and life and between history and the domestic, between universal themes and seemingly trivial detail (though gendered categories all, as we've seen). Indeed, while the series of poems that make up Book Two are given titles suggesting such "universal" themes—Truth, Nature, Passion, Suffering, Death—the poems themselves discuss their themes only briefly and obliquely, offering up fractured details of daily life rather than treatises. Here, by way of example, is the opening of "Chapter Seventy-Seven: Suffering":

> A stench left from cooking fish lay frenzied, felt inert
> Or a yellow rose frustrated in the Summer Garden
> Mayakovsky said that horses never commit suicide because
>   they don't know how to
>   talk—they could never explain their suffering
> Each night has wiped a suffering diagonally—in such
>   conditions each voice and face
>   becomes distorted
> From a neighboring building an infant has been crying for
>   five hours[30]

None of these statements could really be said to apply generally to the "universal" theme of suffering; instead they give us instances of such: a stench, a frustrated bloom, a crying baby. The poem exemplifies precisely the accusation that Romney leveled against Aurora: "You generalize / Oh, nothing,—not even grief! / . . . . The human race / To you means, such a child, or such a man, / You saw one morning waiting in the cold." One could say that Hejinian's poems stand defiantly on the side of "such a child, or such a man," arguing, however, that there is no "human race" but only humans, no generalized pain but only instances of it, just as there are instances of, but no general, redemption:

Chapter Eighty: Redemption

Two rams, which ram redeemed
One ram wasted, one ram waiting [31]

But Hejinian does not only perform gender/genre blending through pointedly drawing together universals and particulars; androgyny and transgender identity also surface directly, and when they do, they are significantly tied to questions of genre. Here is "Chapter 141: The Genders of Everyday Life" in its entirety:

We have split for many occasions
Arkadii!
Ho!
I disagree with you, I said
And I agree, he said—you're right!
About postmodernism
A city of genres
Take a naked doll and a spoon, a lifted city
A great pastiche
You're wrong
I was straightening the blanket around where I sat, while
    Vasya turned up the tape
    machine
An unfinished conspiracy
Love and they are odd—a mounting context
We love the sexes of conditions we never leave. [32]

You will notice that this is the same chapter I quoted from above. But now that we have the title and final lines, we might see how it does more than simply trouble narrative with parataxis and disjunction. We can read this poem now as playfully but significantly exploring the problem of gender division that is at once a problem of genre division.

"We have split for many occasions" begins the poem, and, guided by the title, we read this splitting as, in part, the splitting and dividing of genders (occurring with the splitting and dividing of cells inside the womb). Indeed the "I" (assumed female) and the "he's" are not in much accord; they can't even agree to disagree. The city they argue in, which Hejinain calls "a city of genres," is also, clearly, a city of genders: the naked doll and the spoon both obliquely indicate the female, while Vasya performs a typically "masculine" task, adjusting a machine. The characters cannot be said to have transgressed their gendered roles; indeed, while "he" fiddles with technology, she toys with a feminized object of domestic comfort—a blanket. In fact, in the poem's final line Hejinain remarks on the adherence to "gender law" going on here: "We love the sexes of conditions we never leave." However, remembering Derrida and Butler: only when the "conditions" of gender (or genre) are recognized as such, when such conditions are labeled and performed, can we find "the possibility of contesting [their] reified status."

Indeed, a little while later in *Oxota* we get "a face from which a pronoun is missing," and then the following: "I am not I, said a chalk on the wall / Dickface, said a paint on the door close to cozy / I adore you, my cunt, said Dimitri in English."[33] Here the human is conflated with written or painted surfaces, surfaces that speak, at once rejecting or announcing (exaggeratedly, performatively) their compliance with gendered terms or norms done up crude. Dimitri speaking English reminds us that a "cunt" is only a word; gendered identities are just languages we try on and try out. And while it might seem perverse to read this passage as an instance of gender transgression, I want to take the face with its missing pronoun as the Muse X behind this work. If the political thrust of this "poem–novel" is to resist the oppressive forces of oppositions ("I must oppose the opposition") to break down, just for starters, the Cold War legacy that made enemies of otherness, then these passages reveal how Hejinain must include the dissolving of gendered binaries in her task. In that we have for so long believed (even if subtly) in the myths that gender our genres, *Oxota*, like the other texts we have been looking at, must, in blending the latter, disrupt the former.

"The future calls for perverse crossings," writes Dino Falluga.[34] And while here he means the crossings of genres and periods for literary study, we know that the same is true for gender, as the violence, the sheer brutality of enforced gender compliance becomes more and more evident daily. "Instability marks the site of historical and cultural change,"[35] says Felluga, and in our moment, as America begins, finally, to comprehend that gender is an assignment and not a destiny, as marriage becomes, finally, re- or undefined, we find ourselves standing at the border of a "city of genders" that Barrett Browning could only have dreamed of. As we know, borders are dangerous places, replete with resistance and fear.* But as fissions in the landscape, or in a body—they mark the possible.

Hejinian has the last word: "A boundary is not that at which something stops but, as the Greeks recognized, that from which something *begins*."[36]

*This essay was first written in the summer of 2015. Two years later, facing the "bathroom bill" in North Carolina (and introduced in thirteen other states in 2016 and 2017), the Orlando massacre, and more than fifty reported murders of trans women in the United States in 2015–2016 alone, the danger surrounding gender nonconformity is much more palpable than it felt to me (a cis-woman) then. In 2015 it felt possible to end on a hopeful note. In 2017 it seems an imperative, though a difficult one, to do so.

Notes

1. Jacques Derrida, "The Law of Genre," in *Acts of Literature*, ed. Derek Attridge (New York: Routledge, 1991), 202.

2. Ibid., 225.

3. Ibid., 230.

4. Charles Baudelaire, "The Painter of Modern Life," in *Selected Writings on Art & Artists,* trans. P. E. Charvet (Cambridge: Cambridge University Press, 1972), 430.

5. Judith Butler, "Performative Acts and Gender Constitution: An Essay on Phenomenology and Feminist Theory," *Theater Journal* 40.4 (1988): 520.

6. Dino Felluga, "Novel Poetry: Transgressing the Law of Genre," *Victorian Poetry* 41.4 (Winter 2003): 390.

7. Derrida, "Law of Genre," 245.

8. Ibid., 245.

9. Kazim Ali, "Genre-Queer: Notes Against Generic Binaries," in *Bending Genre: Essays on Creative Nonfiction*, ed. Margot Singer and Nicole Walker (New York: Bloomsbury, 2013), 28–29.

10. The material in this paragraph is repurposed from Julie Carr, *Sur-*

face Tension: Ruptural Time and the Poetics of Desire in Late Victorian Poetry (Champaign, IL: Dalkey Archive, 2013), 122–23.

11. For a more detailed description of these laws and their origins, see Lee Holcombe, *Wives and Property: Reform of the Married Women's Property Law in Nineteenth-Century England* (Toronto: University of Toronto Press, 1983), 18–36. See also Mary Poovey, *Uneven Developments: The Ideological Work of Gender in Mid-Victorian England* (Chicago: University of Chicago Press, 1988), 70–72.

12. Holcombe, *Wives and Property,* 18.

13. Angela Leighton, ed., *Victorian Women Poets: Writing Against the Heart* (Richmond: University of Virginia Press, 1992), 103.

14. Elizabeth Barrett Browning, *Auora Leigh* (New York: W.W. Norton, 1996), 18.

15. Ibid., 44.

16. Ibid., 52.

17. Ibid., 49.

18. Ibid., 45.

19. Murray Krieger, *A Reopening of Closure* (New York: Columbia University Press, 1989), 6–7.

20. Browning, *Auora Leigh,* 148.

21. Williams, *Paterson,* 3.

22. Ibid., 87, 82.

23. Ibid., 217–18.

24. Jacob Edmund, "Bridging Poetic and Cold War Divides in Lyn Hejinain's *Oxota* and Vikram Seth's *Golden Gate,*" 89, accessed May 25, 2017, http://www.enl.auth.gr/gramma/gramma08/edmond.pdf.

25. Marjorie Perloff, "How Russian Is It? Lyn Hejinian's *Oxota,*" accessed May 26, 2017, http://epc.buffalo.edu/authors/perloff/hejin ian.html.

26. Lyn Hejinian, *Oxota: A Short Russian Novel* (Great Barrington, MA: The Figures, 1991), 93.

27. Ibid., 69.

28. Hejinian, "Comments for Manual Brito," in *The Language of Inquiry* (Berkeley: University of California Press, 2000), 182.

29. Hejinian, *A Border Comedy* (New York: Granary Books, 2001), 17.

30. Hejinian, *Oxota,* 88.

31. Ibid., 91.

32. Ibid., 156.

33. Ibid., 192.

34. Felluga, "Novel Poetry," 384.

35. Ibid., 389.

36. Hejinian, *Border,* 18.

Latin for Female Wanderer
On Lisa Robertson

Mostly I seek the promiscuous feeling of being alive.
—Lisa Robertson[1]

At one instant one gets the whole painting. . . . the feeling
is instantaneous, complete. If I succeed in doing that then
I feel I've come close to the true feeling of being alive.
—Barnett Newman[2]

Having spent a few days with one of the poets whose work I have
most lived with and most loved, I find myself faced with a loss
and a gain: "Removed from Accident of Loss / By Accident of
Gain," wrote Dickinson, considering intimacy as an economic
exchange, vulnerable to chance.

I gain a friend, but lose the magic of her voice purely on the
page. As if to compensate, I interview her, recording her voice
so it'll now "sit in my ear" in a new, and newly formalized, way.
And from my chair: a delicate improvisation unfurls raw. It was
good. It was inadequate.

We spoke into the recorder for three hours, and then the
conversation went on into walking, lunch, and the slower and
more interrupted space of an afternoon with kids. Because
Lisa spoke about the improvisatory experience of collaboration
(with Stacy Doris, Alison Clay, and Nathanael especially), about
sociability as an improvisation that opens one to juxtaposition,
the unexpected, and the unplanned, I asked her why she does
not actually improvise in performance, though I wasn't really
sure what I meant by the question.

The night before, I'd had a dream: It is the morning of the day we'd chosen for the interview. I enter the kitchen to find Lisa already dressed (a cute hat and short jacket) and walking out the door. "Where are you going?" I say, a little dismayed, "What about the interview?" But with a distracted wave, she's gone. A bit later, I see her through the kitchen window. She's sitting on the ground under a bush, writing in her notebook. She has friends: a group of circus types, some children, a large bald man. After writing, she spreads a blanket on the ground and lies down to sleep.

Later, the bald man comes into the house, foraging for food. "Did you see a woman," I ask, "out there writing in her notebook?" "Huh?" he says. "No, I don't think so." He's opening cabinets, drawers. I try again: "She's a small woman, in a hat, seated on the ground, writing in a notebook. Maybe she took a nap?" "Oh!" he says. "You mean—." And he says a word that is not English; it's a word I remember from Lisa's books. It might be Italian or Latin, and it means female wanderer. Yes, I say, that's her.

> Where the wanderer is, the conditions of the definite here are lacking. . . . The wanderer's country is not truth, but exile; she lives outside, on the other side which is by no means a beyond, rather the contrary. She remains separated, where the deep of dissimulation reigns, that elemental obscurity through which no way can be made and which because of that makes its awful way through her.[3]

What, I asked Lisa later that day, is Utopia?

The word is a near constant in her work: *The Weather, Magenta Soul Whip, R's Boat, Nilling* . . . all these works take it up.

"My idea of Utopia," she says, "is not that it's an elsewhere, a situated elsewhere to strive toward or that is contained only within an imaginative projection, but that Utopia could be considered more almost in phenomenological terms as a *sensed present.* What I think I mean is that . . . political transformation has to be situated in what we are already in the midst of experiencing." Not, then, some future time of redeemed social life but, instead, a intensification of "now," a transformation that becomes possible when "now-ness" is deeply, as she says, "sensed."[4]

In his 1984 essay, "The Sublime and the Avant-Garde," Jean-Francois Lyotard considers Barnett Newman's paintings as incidents of "the sublime." Newman's stark vertical forms might seem an odd choice—a far cry from Wordsworth's Snowdon, that "emblem of a mind / That feeds upon infinity," but then perhaps not.[5] Pointing to Newman's 1948 essay, "The Sublime is Now," Lyotard explores what the concept of "now" might have to do with the surface textures of Newman's paintings ("the 'it-happens' is the paint," writes Lyotard) and what such "now-ness" might have to do with the term "sublime," so important to Romanticism, to Newman, and to Lyotard.[6]

Tracing Newman's version of the sublime to Burke's (as opposed to Kant's) theory, Lyotard argues that what Newman is after, what he means by "sublime," *is* the aesthetic representation of this "now-ness." Thus Newman's title, "The Sublime is Now," takes "is" as a verb of equivalence and "now" as an abstract concept rather than a specific moment in time (May of 1948, for example). Aesthetic objects, writes Lyotard, that work to represent this feeling of "now-ness" create in their viewers what he calls an "ontological dislocation," a disturbing but exhilarating sense that the self is unknowable to itself. In trying to "present the fact" of the "unpresentable" *now*, the work of art offers the viewer a dismantling but ultimately transforming experience, more disruptive but also more productive than the comforting experience of "beauty."[7] "What kind of time was Newman concerned with, what 'now' did he have in mind?" asks Lyotard. Not just the "fleeting" present, he argues, but instead a "now-ness" that "is a stranger to consciousness and cannot be constituted by it." This sense of now, says Lyotard, "is what dismantles consciousness, what deposes consciousness, it is what consciousness cannot formulate, and even what consciousness forgets in order to constitute itself."[8]

I want to be sure to underline that for Lyotard the apprehension of "now-ness" is a transformative experience; when time's ongoing flow is ruptured by a perceived sense of "now" made accessible through an encounter with a work of art, the experience for the viewer or reader is shocking. But this shock is not without benefits. Breaking out of habitually sensed chronological time "must inspire the wonderful surprise, the wonder that there should be something rather than nothing." Presence, Lyotard writes, "is the instant which interrupts the chaos of history and which recalls, or simply calls out that 'there is.'"[9]

As in the biblical or rabbinical renditions of this concept of immediacy, of truly "sensed" presence, we find in Lyotard's response to Newman a kind of *rapture*—"a painting by Newman is an angel."[10] It performs an annunciation, but what it announces is simply presence itself. The verb "to be" becomes its own Utopic utterance.

"Utopia is so emotional" begins the second section of Robertson's poem "A Hotel," from her 2005 book *Lisa Robertson's Magenta Soul Whip.* Then:

> I'm speaking of the pure sexual curves
> Of Utopia, the rotation
> Of its shadows against the blundering
> In civitas[11]

Utopia casts its erotically charged shadow across the present as if it's simply an "other life" sliding across or perhaps under this one. And yet, the "Big problem of poetry," as she suggests a few lines later, is *how* to evoke this redeemed time, how to gesture toward the redeemed moment, while immersing oneself in the here-and-now sensations of the text. "On this very beautiful surface / Where I want to live / I play with my friends," she writes. But this admission of textual pleasure is not a rejection of urgency; quite the opposite: "I believe my critique of devastation / Began with delight. Now what surprises me / Are the folds of political desire / Their fragile nobility, Sundays of / Rain."

Critique begins and ends not with analysis, not with suffering, but with pleasure, the pleasures of the social, the pleasures of the poem, the pleasures of the body in the present. Pleasure stands in resistance, one could say, to all forms of oppression, to those that deny the body its freedoms, to those that seek to make ascetics out of all of us (hoarders and misers), and to those that insist we grow accustomed to pain and suffering inflicted, if not directly upon us, then on so many near to us and in our name. Thus the poem, as a surface dedicated to pleasure ("Some think only of pleasure in their projects / I am one of those people / . . . I'll solicit nothing / But ornament"), is already a form of critique. Nonetheless, the tension between the pleasures of the text and the "political desire" for a redeemed social space is palpable in this poem, forcing it into the mode of a defense, though a soft one. Perhaps this hint of self-implication or doubt provides the "whip" of *Magenta Soul Whip.* And yet, again and again in Robertson's work, sensation itself—ornament, pleasure, bodily experience—are offered as the means toward an intensified experience of "now," and such an experience *is* the redeemed or "utopian" moment, even if felt only in flashes.

The long poem titled "Utopia," which appears in *R's Boat*,[12] is specifically concerned with the relationship between present-time and utopian renewal. "I wanted to study the ground, the soft ruins of paper and the rusting things," Robertson writes. "I discovered a tenuous utopia made from steel, wooden chairs, glass, stone, metal bed frames, tapestry, bones, prosthetic legs, hair, shirt cuffs, nylon, plaster figurines, perfume bottles and keys." Poetry, in its propensity to name, to gather, to engage language as thing, is a kind of scavenger hunt performed by the poet in the present and on the ground. Or Utopia is precisely this act of gathering, studying, observing, this act of engaging the present with one's sensations on alert. "Women," she writes, "from a settlement called Utopia focus on the intricate life that exists there." And then later, "What we are proposing already exists."

The poem presents time, the marking of time, as its central preoccupation. All but one of its eighteen stanzas open with a reference to a date or season: "In the Spring of 1979"; "The season called November"; "At about midnight in Autumn"; "At about four in the morning, that first day"; "It is late October"; and so on. And yet, no chronology organizes these references; rather, time seems to be spiraling around itself. Further, even as the months and seasons might want to pull us into past or future, the paratactic (and present-tense) mode of Robertson's sentences brings us into present-time experience again and again: "Pollen smears the windows. / The blackberry vines are Persian. / The boulder smells faintly of warm sugar." These sensual present-time descriptions remind us too of the pleasures of surface: the smear on a windowpane, the scent on the surface of a stone. "The day shows a licked surface," and earlier, "The face moves across the human." The face here, like the shadows of Utopia in "A Hotel," becomes a surface that holds the potential for what I can only call redemption, as I'm reminded not only of Lyotard but also of Benjaminian now-time. To quote Benjamin scholar Stéphane Mosès: for Benjamin and Gershom Sholem, "utopia [is] a function of the experience of the present."[13]

> [F]or Benjamin and Scholem . . . Utopia, which can no longer be thought of as belief in the necessary advent of the ideal at the mythical end of history, reemerges—through the category of Redemption—as the modality of its possible advent at each moment in time. In this model of random time, open at any moment to the unpredictable eruption of the new, the imminent realization of the ideal becomes conceivable again, as one of the possibilities offered by the unfathomable complexity of historical processes.
>
> . . .
>
> [T]he idea of "now-time" . . . that idea inspired by Jewish messianism, proposes a model of history that, after the collapse of the ideologies of progress, gives a new chance for hope by locating utopia in the heart of the present.[14]

"What we are proposing," writes Robertson in "Utopia," "already exists."

Despite how the paratactic mode of the poem seems to defer resolution, as the poem moves on we do find Robertson's "Utopia" beginning to take form. As she puts it, "Quietly, a shape becomes noticeable." A fantastical version of the self (with a dog's legs and a fish's tail) drifts by a train window; "girls chat in trees about the mystical value of happiness"; other girls pick fruit.

The poem's final words, set off on their own page and in larger font (so that the couplet might be its own poem), read: "This Is the Beginning of Utopia / Its Material is Time." The poem's final image is of a decaying reading chair set out of doors:

> At the periphery of the overgrown clearing, the skeleton of a
> reading chair
> decaying beneath plastic.

Perhaps any vision of redemption, of utopian renewal, must include not only present-time sensation but also some idea of decay or destruction. Further, utopian hopes and the practice of reading, the practice, one could say, of *poetry*, are deeply entwined. That these activities should happen in an exterior space, an "overgrown clearing," speaks back to a line from the first page of "Utopia": "Any girl who reads is already a lost girl." To be lost, to be a wanderer, is a kind of freedom in other times only available to men: "Now I am free, enfranchised and at large / I fix my habitation where I will," wrote Wordsworth in *The Prelude* and later, "I, too, have been a wanderer."[15] In our time, for a woman this is still a position of resistance.

In early 2017 Robertson presented a talk at the Edinburgh College of Art titled "Proverbs of a She-Dandy."[16] Here she takes the Baudelairian concept of the dandy (as described in his "The Painter of Modern Life") and applies it to the menopausal woman. The menopausal woman, argues Robertson, holds and presents the wealth of her own autonomy. Outside of capital's demand for productivity, she is, like the dandy, free to wander in her own pleasures:

> SHE IS THE MASTERPIECE OF THE ANCIENT SUPERI-
> ORITY OF THE IMPRODUCTIVE. SHE NEITHER BEGETS
> NOR WORKS, BUT DRIFTS.
>
> . . .
>
> WEALTH IS THE AUTONOMOUS EXPERIENCE OF ONE'S
> OWN PLEASURE, A FLAWED PLEASURE INNATE TO EM-
> BODIMENT. MOVING EXTREMELY SLOWLY ON THE
> BOULEVARD, IN THE PARK, AT THE NEWS STAND, IN
> THE BOOKSHOP, SHE DISPLAYS HER RESISTANCE TO
> ALL APPROPRIATION SAVE THE POEM'S.

The talk makes use of the term "resistance" more than once. Earlier, "HER OBSOLESCENCE IS INDISPENSIBLE TO HER WORK WITH RESISTANCE." At the moment when the reproductive imperative can no longer apply, the free-moving power of the autonomous body can surge.

When I woke from the dream in which Lisa abandoned the house to write in a clearing (and in which I was within the house, cleaning), I reached for her new book *Nilling* and read the following two passages:

> In heavy and worthy houses, I feel a violent dismay. It gets harder and harder to be female in one's life in such a house. What has commodiousness become? I abandon the house for the forbidden book.

> Something can change. The dispersed rhythm of wandering—musical and conceptual—is what its folds conduct. Rhythm is a figured, embodied improvisation, not a measure.[17]

Here, again, is Blanchot on the topic (please forgive, disregard, abstract, or resist pronouns here):

> Exile, the poem then, makes the poet a wanderer, the one always astray, he to whom the stability of presence is not granted and who is deprived of a true abode.

> And this must be understood in the gravest sense: the artist does not belong to truth because the work is itself what escapes the movement of the true, eludes signification, designating that region where nothing subsists, where what takes place has nevertheless never taken place, where what begins over has never begun. . . . The eternal outside is quite well evoked by the image of the *exterior* darkness where man understands that which the true must negate in order to become possible and to progress.[18]

The value of the wanderer, the exile, lies in her residence, which is outside, in the wilds, the unstable, and the unlocatable anywhere, where possibility dwells.

The evening after our interview Lisa gives a reading at the University of Denver. She begins by describing our day together: flowers, kids, conversation. And then she mentions what I'd said: "Why not just improvise?" She presents my question as a challenge. "And so," she goes on, "not just to prove to Julie that I can, I will improvise this reading from my notebook."

She reads from a large book fluidly, as if the poem is already constructed, always has been. There are pauses while she flips pages at random, selecting new material to begin and begin again ("we are satisfied, we are happy, / we begin again"—H.D. *Trilogy*[19]).

"The new beginning inherent in birth can make itself felt in the world only because the newcomer possesses the capacity of beginning something anew, that is, of acting," writes Hannah Arendt, the "theorist of beginning," and one of Lisa's primary guides.[20]

Improvisation makes a softening. It makes a rhythm out of thinking. As she reads I write with one hand on my daughter's knee to keep her from rustling, and I'm unsure which of these words I heard, which came from the elsewhere that is "my" mind. ("Plurality is *the* [human] condition," says Arendt.[21] "Identity can't be concise. It's knit from sequence and lust and scatters," writes Lisa in *Magenta Soul Whip*.[22])

> Lilac presses its scent as we walk across the street holding hands with the girl, carrying the shoeless smaller one, on the summer not yet summer night. Crescent moon low in a clarity. It was good. It was inadequate. We were eating boiled flowers. Were we running from our own bodies, making of health a project?

> She delays form. She puts form on an infinite track. *I cried for death in general.* Dancers with their hands on the floor, a line between their brows, concentrate on time and how it passes.

> I've had the good luck to be a bow. For an arrow. Under a cherry tree in full bloom. An absurd and burning optimism. It

was good, but only April, and everything in the garden made me fear it.

A utopian poetics, a utopian *practice*, grounded in the specific pleasures of present-time sensation seeks only and outrageously "the promiscuous feeling of being alive."[23]

Notes

1. Robertson, *Nilling*, 12.

2. Lane Slate, "Barnett Newman," 16-mm film, National Education Television, 1966.

3. Maurice Blanchot, *The Space of Literature*, trans. Anne Smock (Lincoln: University of Nebraska Press, 1989), 238.

4. Julie Carr, "An Interview with Lisa Robertson," accessed October 25, 2017: http://www.thevolta.org/ewc25-jcarr-p1.html.

5. Wordsworth, *The Prelude*, XIV:70–71.

6. Jean-Francois Lyotard, "The Sublime and the Avant-Garde," in *The Inhuman: Reflections in Time*, trans. Geoffrey Bennington (Palo Alto, CA: Stanford University Press, 1992), 93.

7. Ibid., 101.

8. Ibid., 90. "Here then is an account of the sublime feeling: a very big, very powerful object threatens to deprive the soul of any 'it happens,' strikes it with astonishment. . . . The soul is thus dumb, immobilized, as good as dead. Art, by distancing this menace, procures a pleasure of relief, of delight. Thanks to art, the soul is returned to the agitated zone between life and death, and this agitation is its health and its life. For Burke, the sublime was no longer a matter of elevation . . . but a matter of intensification." Ibid., 100.

9. Ibid., 85, 87.

10. Ibid., 79.

11. Robertson, *Lisa Robertson's Magenta Soul Whip* (Toronto: Coach House Books, 2005), 18–21.

12. Robertson, *R's Boat* (Berkeley: University of California Press, 2010), 49–68.

13. Stéphane Mosès, *The Angel of History: Rosenzweig, Benjamin, Scholem*, trans. Barbara Harshav (Stanford, CA: Stanford University Press, 2009), 125.

14. Ibid., 12–13, 14.

15. Wordsworth, *The Prelude*, I:6–15, XI:252.

16. Robertson, "Proverbs of a She-Dandy," accessed May 25, 2017, http://buenostiemposinternational.com/lisa-robertson_13–4-2017/.

17. Robertson, *Nilling*, 15.

18. Blanchot, *Literature*, 237–38.

19. H.D., *Trilogy*, 109.

20. Hannah Arendt, *The Human Condition*, 9.

21. Ibid., 8.

22. Robertson, *Magenta Soul Whip*, 89.

23. Robertson, *Nilling*, 12.

On Saying No

Valentine and Dickinson Break the Glass

Don't listen to the words
They're only little shapes for what you're saying
They're only cups if you're thirsty, you aren't thirsty

So ends the poem "As with rosy steps the morn" from Jean Valentine's 2012 collection, *Break the Glass.* The poem is an elegy of sorts for soprano Lorraine Hunt Lieberson; its opening lines evoke a world beyond, on the other side, of this one: "Everyone on the reverse of the picture / on the other side of the measuring eye."[1] The measuring eye is bound to the material world, the world of objects, of immanence (immancence, coming from Latin, means to remain within). In its second stanza the poem moves to describe a musical expression:

> The five notes, slowly, over & over
> and with some light intent,
> And the whole air,
> no edge, no center,
>
> And the light so thin, so fast—

Valentine is not often a punning poet, but here the word "light" holds both of its meanings—the musical phrase is nearly weightless (like a Valentine poem) and also intended toward the light, toward transcendence, toward the spirit. "Air" too carries two meanings—both a song and a gas—as music becomes spirit or God of the air: without edge, without center. Less obviously, the "notes" of the stanza's first line can refer at once to musical notes and to written ones—letters, or notes in a notebook, or perhaps the gestures of a poem. This way, even as the poem offers music as a kind of gateway to spiritual life, it also aligns music with writing (especially when we notice that the poem's first stanza holds just five lines, five "notes"). But if writing, or musical language—poetry—can carry us, by way of its "light intent" into the "reverse of the picture," toward contact with the spirit, we can look now again to the end of this poem to see the tension at the center of this hope. For words themselves are for Valentine "only little shapes for what you're saying"; they are "cups"—matter, mere objects—and what they hold will not quench your truest thirst. The most obvious referent for that final "you" is Lorraine Hunt Lieberson herself; she's no longer thirsty because no longer living. But allowing that "you" can also refer to the reader and as easily to the poet, then the final lines remind us to look beyond the meaning of words, beyond what they "say" and toward, it seems, their musical function in order to hear in them "the whole air," the voice, one could say (and I think Valentine would say), of God.[2]

As crucial as this turning toward, or *tuning* toward, the "whole air" becomes here, it's *as* crucial to notice that in order to turn toward, Valentine's poems suggest that one first must turn away—must reject or refuse a certain set of desires ("don't listen to the words") in order to open to spiritual life. This could be the driving force behind all of Valentine's work, especially her more recent work—the act of refusal that is, in fact, an opening, a deep receptivity. Valentine's quiet minimalism is a way to prepare for, to make space for, a greater, more maximal, engagement. Here are some other instances from *Break the Glass* in which Valentine turns away, says no, or suggests a rejection or refusal:

> don't read this yet,
> my thoughts are still packed down
> like crumpled letters, and some of us
> will not get quite free—
> > —"Dear Family"

> your blackwater embrace-
> not bought or sold.
> > —"The Japanese Garden"

You can't get beauty. (Still,
   in its longing it flies to you.)
      —"Then Abraham"

but not hunger
   or hunger not granted
      —"(Two were seen leaving)"

   —life from whom
death also springeth green
   —thy leave to sleep
      —"The just-born rabbits"

I put my hand on the ground
the membrane is gone
and nothing does hold
   —"Red cloth"

I never thirst
   —"Eurydice who guides"[3]

When Valentine does affirm, when she moves toward rather than away, she directs herself or her speakers toward some rendition of spiritual life, the afterlife perhaps—though one hesitates to adopt teleology. Here are just three examples from the book of this "turning toward": "Ghost elephant, / reach down, / cross me over"; "Break the glass shout / Break the glass force the room / break the thread Open / the music behind the glass"; "Do we get another life? *Oh yes. / Maybe not in this place. Maybe in a different form.*"[4] Clearly Valentine's work is not "negative" in its mood. Rather, in the moments of negation lie deeper moments of affirmation. As she writes, "not that I am drawn to that which withdraws / but to him *pearled, asleep,* who never withdraws."[5]

Yet even in this last instance, we sense that the sought after "him," though described as always available, must remain hidden (like a pearl), must be approached cautiously as one would approach a sleeper. I'm reminded here of another contemporary metaphysical poet, one very close to Valentine personally and poetically, Fanny Howe, who offers the following: "One definition of the lyric might be that it is a method of searching for something that can't be found. It is an air that blows and buoys and settles. It says, 'Not this, not this,' instead of, 'I have it.'"[6] (Interestingly, Howe uses "air" here to describe the poem, and her "air" too has "no edge, no center," as it restlessly searches.) But one can also trace Valentine's use of negative constructions to a source at once more distant and more near, Emily Dickinson. Here is one well-known moment of Dickinsonian negation that I think reveals the intimacy between these two poets:

259.
A Clock stopped—
Not the Mantel's
Geneva's farthest skill
Cant put the puppet bowing—
That just now dangled still—

An awe came on the Trinket!
The Figures hunched—with pain—
Then quivered out of Decimals—
Into Degreeless noon—

It will not stir for Doctor's—
This Pendulum of snow—
The Shopman importunes it—
While cool—concernless No—

Nods from the Gilded pointers—
Nods from the Seconds slim—
Decades of Arrogance between
The Dial life—
And Him—

The poem imagines the end of ordinary "measured" or numerical (decimal) time (remember Valentine's "measuring eye"), evoking the biblical apocalypse.[7] The clock is simply a "trinket" belonging to the profane realms of commerce and adornment, but when "stopped," it becomes itself adorned, adorned with awe, for now in its stillness it measures eternity.[8] The figures (either those figurines that might come out to dance when the clock strikes the hour or the numbers themselves) metaphorically suggest the souls awaiting judgment at the moment of Christ's second coming. And yet, in order for this revelation to occur, something else has to end—and that something else is what Dickinson calls, with indelible accuracy, "The Dial life," time itself. However, as often in Dickinson's poems, the moment of spiritual revelation is also the moment of writing. ("Emily Dickinson's religion was poetry," writes Susan Howe.[9]) For the referent in the third stanza, the "it" that resists the aid of doctor and shopman (standing here as defenders of the life of the body, of commerce and town) is not only the broken clock with its frozen pendulum; it's also the poet, or more directly, the poem. As we know, Dickinson used "snow" as a metaphor for her writing, and thus the poem's pendulum-like rhythms create a different kind of time, which, unlike "the Dial life," does not stand arrogantly at a remove from God. Instead, it stands coolly unconcerned before the ordinary secular world. In rejecting the entreaties of doctor and shopman, the "snow" affirms "Him."

Two other poems from *Break the Glass*, "Eurydice who guides" and "He Disappeared into Complete Silence,"[10] provide powerful examples of negation functioning to affirm spiritual commitment. "Eurydice who guides" takes on the familiar myth by unconventionally giving agency to Eurydice herself, acknowledging her role as guide rather than positioning her as only the object of Orpheus's desire. Here Eurydice is not simply the lost beloved; she is emblematic of death itself. Orpheus's pursuit is less that of a lover and more that of the poet compelled to confront the question of mortality. In this sense Valentine's "reading" of the myth resembles that of Blanchot. But even in Blanchot, who sees Orpheus's descent *and* his glance back at Eurydice as metaphors for the artist's calling, his "impulse" or "demand," Eurydice herself has no agency. She is the poet's desire, his need to confront the invisible (the "essence of the night"), or she is the work itself.[11] For Valentine, however, death and poetry (or Eurydice and Orpheus) find themselves in a kind of tango (not unlike that between Dickinson's "loaded gun" and its master).[12] If the poet attempts to draw close, it's equally true that death compels the poet to follow:

> Eurydice who guides   Orpheus who guides
> who first has to return to death
> the one who sings
> the one who opens first

Orpheus's singing allows him to "return to death," to retrieve Eurydice, but she, in crossing over into the underworld, has "opened" first. Perhaps. The pronoun "one" in lines 3 and 4 is ambiguous, and I think meaningfully so. It's not ultimately decidable which of the lovers is the "one who sings," which is "the one who opens first." They guide one another, neither leads, neither follows. Valentine then takes this idea further, imagining Eurydice and Orpheus as mutually mothering, mutually nurturing: "his / mouth to her song / her thirst his thirst / the ones who nurse each other."

This moment echoes an earlier poem of Valentine's, "Mare and Newborn Foal":

> When you die
> there are bales of hay
> heaped high in space
> mean while
> with my tongue
> I draw the black straw
> out of you
> mean while
> with your tongue
> you draw the black straw out of me.[13]

This "black straw" is at once a metaphor for life—milk—and for death—the spirit or soul exiting the body (the poem recalls Celan's "black milk"). Mother and infant guide each other toward death by way of nurturing. In "Eurydice who guides" too, what might be the ultimate negation—death itself—is instead equal to the essential (for the poet) opening, the opening that is song: "his / mouth to her song."

I'm reminded here of Nathaniel Mackey's deeply moving essay, "Sound and Sentiment, Sound and Symbol," in which Mackey asserts that, "music or poetry, if not exactly a loser's art, is fed by an intimacy with loss and may in fact feed it."[14] Mackey argues that poetry's *political* force emerges from its ability to confront, to sing about, absence, loss, or breaches in kinship. For Valentine too there's no contradiction between the poem that is intimate with death, that expresses a dedication to the life of the spirit, and the poem that confronts real-world injustice, real-world suffering. "Song is both a complaint and a consolation dialectically tied to [the ordeal of the orphan], where in back of 'orphan' one hears echoes of 'orphic,' a music that turns on abandonment, absence, loss," writes Mackey.[15] For Mackey, the condition of the "orphan" is not simply existential (though it is), it is also political—a condition brought about by institutional and personal racism ("music is wounded kinship's last resort"). Similarly for Valentine, the poem that, by way of negation, seeks to affirm the "reverse of the picture," the "other side," does so not only out of spiritual yearning but also out of political outrage (such as in the intensely moving "In Prison," which opens this volume).

In the final lines of "Eurydice who guides," after we witness the mutual nursing of death and poetry, we are granted the comforting voice of, amazingly, a "blackened saucepan"—figure of both sustenance and ash:

> Don't be afraid the blackened saucepan said
> I met them in the country by the well
> and once I drank from them
> I never thirsted

To "never thirst" is, in this poem, to be quenched by both death and poetry. But the joining of the two marks not the cessation of life but rather the opening into the other life. Again, Dickinson:

> 61.
> My foot is in the Tide!
> An unfrequented road—
> Yet have all roads
> A clearing at the end—

> 119.
> If this is "fading"
> O let me immediately "fade"!

> If this is "dying"
> Bury—me, in such a shroud of red!

I'll conclude with Valentine's "He Disappeared into Complete Silence," another poem in which a negation (here as silence) is presented in order to affirm its opposite, in this case, speech.

> The wild ladders of longing
> no longer pieces of wild wood, sawed off
> and fitted to each other,
> no longer stored in a closed-off room
> with one blank window
> But called back, through
> the closed-off wooden ceiling, to his
> speech returned.

This poem imagines a kind of spiritual death as a "closed-off room," a prison of sorts with its "one blank window." But as the "ladders of longing" (the immanent object) are transformed into the "calling" (the transcendent voice), the silence of the title emerges as "speech returned." As in Dickinson's work, we can read this "calling" as at once the voice of God and as that other calling, the calling of the poet (or, more broadly, the artist, since this poem is an ekphrastic response to Louise Bourgeois's "plate 8" from 1947). "Called back," the spirit moves upward through the wooden ceiling into speech again; the silenced body is answered with the voice of the spirit.

On the wall above Valentine's writing desk is a framed rubbing of Dickinson's grave, a rubbing Valentine did herself. The gravestone gives Dickinson's name, dates, and the words "Called Back." Even in this simple phrase (which Dickinson chose for her own epitaph) we hear the shadow of a negation, an Orphic turning toward that is at once a turning away. Seeking beauty, thirsting, hungering—these energies of striving will not, in Valentine's work, deliver us to (spiritual) beauty or nourishment. Instead, as in the poem "The Young Mother," we advance in a metaphysical process by, in a sense, "withholding" from such efforts: "All you people looking out from the stern / of the white ship *Withholding* //—I'll take my babies and swim."[16] Perhaps one could say that Dickinson is on that ship, *is* that ship. With her one foot in the tide, she advances across time, as if effortlessly called back to Valentine. Or perhaps we could as readily say that this ship is poetry itself, which we cannot advance upon but, instead, must be willing to receive.

> Ambition cannot find him—
>   Dickinson, 115

> You can't get beauty. (Still,
> in its longing it flies to you.)
>   Valentine, "Then Abraham"[17]

Notes

1. Jean Valentine, *Break the Glass* (Port Townsend, WA: Copper Canyon Press, 2012), 10.

2. The poem is referencing Lieberson's aria as Irene in Handel's oratorio *Theodora*.

3. Valentine, *Break the Glass*, 11, 13, 16, 29, 31, 35, 40.

4. Ibid., 14, 42, 50.

5. Ibid., 42.

6. Fanny Howe, *The Wedding Dress: Meditations on Word and Life* (Berkeley: University of California Press, 2003), 21.

7. Dickinson's second letter to Higginson of April 25, 1862, reads, "For poets—I have Keats and Mr. and Mrs. Browning. For prose—Mr. Ruskin, Sir Thomas Browne, and the Revelations." Emily Dickinson, *Selected Letters,* ed. Thomas H. Johnson (Cambridge, MA: Belknap Press, 1958, 1971, 1986), 404.

8. "Circumference thou Bride of Awe," she writes in a late poem (1636). "I always ran Home to Awe when a child," she wrote to Higginson in 1874. Dickinson, Selected *Letters,* 517.

9. Susan Howe, *My Emily Dickinson* (New York: New Directions, 2007), 48.

10. Valentine, *Break the Glass*, 40, 52.

11. Blanchot, *Gaze,* 100.

12. Thus Valentine's poem resembles more closely the reading of the Orpheus/Eurydice myth that Kaja Silverman develops in *Flesh of My Flesh* in which Eurydice becomes the central figure, drawing Orpheus to confront his own finitude and thus his (our) connection to all other finite things.

13. Valentine, *Door in the Mountain: New and Collected Poems, 1965–2003* (Middletown, CT: Wesleyan University Press, 2007), 250.

14. Mackey, *Discrepant Engagement,* 240.

15. Ibid., 232.

16. Valentine, *Break the Glass,* 46.

17. Ibid., 16.

Women and War, Love, Labor
The Legacy of Lorine Niedecker

The title for this essay came to me in a dream. I was a student
in a class on feminism. The teacher was political philosopher
Wendy Brown. We were looking at images of the second-wave
feminist movement—women marching together, waving signs,
chanting slogans, looking amazing in their T-shirts and sunglass-
es. It's not like that anymore, someone said sadly. What do we
do now? Brown agreed—It's not, she said, for us to fight a war
now. To be a feminist in America now one must turn to labor
and to love.

I know what my dreaming self thought Brown meant: that
we have to labor regularly and doggedly for the equality and
safety of women, not just here but everywhere. It won't be a glo-
rious battle; it will be work, and like all work it will be hard and
sometimes frustrating, confusing, and dull. At the same time,
we have to "learn to love" (the title of an interview with Brown
I'd just finished reading was "Learning to Love Again"). This
means we have to learn more about what love means for us in
the personal/political sphere(s). We have to learn how to struc-
ture a society grounded in love, which is to say, in desire and
vulnerability and care. (This second point is how I understood
the recent work of Brown's partner, Judith Butler.)

But the irony was not lost on me while dreaming, nor when
awake. Love and (certain kinds of) labor have always been with-
in "women's domain." Not just the labor of birthing, though
that comes immediately to mind, but also domestic labor, fac-
tory labor, farm labor, office labor, teaching labor, healing la-
bor: all the laboring that women have done and still do, often
under-recognized, unpaid or underpaid, often while caring for

children, sometimes without much or any help from those children's fathers or (at least in the US) from the state.

And love—we know that (heterosexual) "love" and its ideologies have, throughout history, often stood as barriers to the freedoms of women and girls under patriarchy, which is why when my then five-year-old said, with a slightly theatrical spreading of her arms, "Love is the most important thing!" I winced a bit.

But, I would argue, it's precisely because of these ironies, because of the way that "love" and "labor" have so often meant forms of oppression for women, that Wendy Brown is telling me to think about these terms, to reignite them in some way—and it's precisely because of the relationship they bear to war and violence too.

This essay is about the legacy of Lorine Niedecker, a poet often thought of in terms of labor—for famously, unlike many well-known poets of all generations, she was not financially well-off, nor was she supported by an academic or professional job. And unlike many of the middle- and upper-class women of her generation, she was not supported by a male partner either. She worked—first as a proofreader, later as a manager of modest vacation properties she'd inherited, and finally, as a cleaning woman. Moreover, she wrote often about labor and class, about the daily tasks of laundry, lawn mowing, wood chopping, and cooking, and also writing—about the ways in which class differences assert themselves in our streets and homes. As Margaret Ronda puts it, "Niedecker center[s] [her] poetics on a structuring concept of *labor* as animating force governing social processes, forms of bodily being and knowing, and aesthetic creations."[1]

Less often noted, but as predominantly, Niedecker was a poet of war. As Eleni Sikelianos writes, "Lorine Niedecker . . . quietly recorded the presence of things that fly through the air and explode in body and mind." Sikelianos finds "the disjunctiveness of a world gone to war" not only in the references to wounded, dismembered soldiers, or to blasts, gasses, and bombs (the London Blitz, the atom bomb), but also in the pieced together forms of Niedecker's long poems. Sikelianos suggests that Niedecker reaches toward a kind of healing of the ruptured world by way of form, as her serial poems construct "wholes" out of severed parts.[2]

Not only is Niedecker a poet of labor and a poet of war (her two most frequently used nouns are "war" and "work," reports Elizabeth Willis), she's also a poet of the intimate relationship between the two.[3] She understood the soldier as a worker and understood too the ways that capitalism depends on war as one of its most productive industries, even as its human cost is paid out primarily by the poor. In poems such as "Bombings," "Tell me a story about the war," and "1937," she reveals this damaging dynamic. And when she pairs such poems as "They came at a pace" with "I doubt I'll get silk stocking out" (*New Goose*) or "The number of Briton's killed" with "Old Hamilton hailed the man from the grocery story" (*New Goose Manuscript*), she seems to be using proximity to speak to the ways war and labor (or class) intertwine.

But how does one speak of "love" in Niedecker's work? The subject of romantic love, at least, seems more often avoided than explored. Rather, Niedecker is nothing short of sardonic in her assessment of gender relations, whether she's considering the ways girls present themselves as objects of desire "with their bottoms out" ("Not feeling well") or thinking about the subjection of women in marriage, such as in the poem "So you're married young man," where she writes, "She needs washers and dryers / she needs bodice uplift / she needs deep-well cookers / she needs power shift," or in "I rose from marsh mud," where she describes a bride as a "little white slave girl / in her diamond fronds." Despite the loving gesture of her "For Paul" poems (and perhaps through the child to the father), there is very little even here of direct expressions of love or affection.[4]

So how *does* love show up in Niedecker's work, and how might this "love" be a response to the destructions of war she is so keenly aware of throughout her career? Interestingly, love becomes thematized most directly in Niedecker's "handmade" projects, projects that were also, not incidentally, gifts, two of which bookend her career: *NEXT YEAR OR I FLY MY ROUNDS, TEMPESTUOUS* (mid-1930s, for Zukofsky) and *Homemade Poems* (1964, for Cid Corman). Indeed, we often refer to handmade objects as "labors of love." They take so much time—"unnecessary" time, since a machine could usually do it quicker—that one has to "love" the work to bother with it. But also, homemade objects speak directly of intimacy, for they bear the mark of their maker's hands as they reach toward a receiver. These works are "labors of love" in a third way too: not only does the handmade object resist the numbing and distancing effects of capitalist production, but also handmade work becomes for Niedecker, as for many poets who have followed her, a way to resist the estrangements and destructions of war and other forms of violence.

Before we look at examples of this dynamic in Niedecker's work, I'd like to gesture to the present by talking briefly about the contemporary phenomenon labeled "craftivism." Craftivism, as the name implies, is a form of activism rooted in craftwork. Needlepoint, knitting, bookmaking, sewing, these traditionally female activities, have been reclaimed by contemporary often female artists who see in that work an opportunity for resistance. Such resistance functions on various levels and has various targets. Craftivism often stands against patriarchal aspects of the art world (and thus, by extension, of culture in general), which has traditionally devalued the aesthetic labor of women throughout history. It stands more generally, and perhaps wishfully, against global capitalism's factory-made objects and the objectification of the human that capital enables.[5] For the crafter, the handmade object resists the "commodification of all aspects of life"[6] not only because it offers a non-alienated form of labor but also because it invents a new/old temporality, a slow-time that is in itself a transformed mode of life. As Anne Cvetkovitch writes, "the craft of slow living . . . take[s] up the manual labor often associated with working-class and precapitalist ways of living and working. . . . As a practice, and not just an ephemeral feeling, crafting is not the homology or first step or raw material for some form of political change beyond it. It is already a form of self-transformation."[7]

But significantly, craftivists have also often brought their work to bear directly on war and its ravages, as a form of art-as-protest. As Kirsty Robertson writes, describing the works of several female artists:

> In the work of artists such as Barb Hunt of Canada and Maria Porges of New York, antiwar statements are made through the juxtaposition of the softness and warmth of wool with

the form of bombs, guns, and landmines. Both artists knit or felt weaponry out of pastel-colored wool. The Toronto artist Barbara Todd makes quilts out of suit fabric in the shape of fighter jets to demonstrate the links between capitalism and the military, while the Dutch artist Marianne Jorensen organized a collaborative project to make a bright pink tea cozy for a military tank [*Pink Tank*].[8]

Some of this work, such as *Pink Tank*, the work of the Revolutionary Knitting Circle, the post-Newtown anti–gun violence group Moms Demand Action, which early on urged its members to make T-shirts, mugs, hats, and other handmade objects as a way to voice opposition to lax or absent gun control laws, or even more recently, the organizers of the 2017 Women's March who encouraged marchers to knit and wear "pussy hats," emphasizes the collaborative and democratic nature of crafting, while placing "textiles . . . at the forefront of a political practice."[9] In these works, the handmade thing, despite or because of its often soft, delicate, small, and intimate qualities, directly opposes militarized violence.[10]

In thinking about the labor of love as anti-war document in Niedecker's work, it's important to look back as well as forward. Elizabeth Willis has written at length about Niedecker's affiliation with William Morris and the Arts and Crafts movement he founded at the end of the nineteenth century. Willis traces that affiliation in Niedecker's letters and especially in the poem Niedecker wrote about Morris in 1969, "His Carpets Flowered." As Willis notes, the Arts and Crafts movement (unlike its development as high-end furnishing and design in early twentieth-century California) "shifted the paradigm of art production in several important ways."[11] Like the craftivist movement of today, the Arts and Crafts movement helped to dissolve boundaries between high and low art, between such things as knitting, weaving, embroidery, and furniture making and such activities as painting and verse writing. Furthermore, Morris, like John Ruskin before him, tied the labor of craft, aesthetic labor of all kinds, directly to the liberation of the maker and thus to a utopian vision of redeemed social life. In this vision, articulated in Morris's utopian novel *News from Nowhere,* all people will be involved only in what Morris called the "difficult easy labor" of working physically and with creative faculties fully engaged in a barter economy freed from the exploitations of industrial capitalism.

Morris thus draws a direct link between the handmade object and the liberation of people from what he called the "continuous and unresting" "war" of the class system. As he wrote in his 1883 lecture, "Art Under Plutocracy":

> [T]hat system [capitalism] is after all nothing but a continuous implacable war; the war once ended, commerce, as we now understand the word, comes to an end, and the mountains of wares which are either useless in themselves or only useful to slaves and slave-owners are no longer made, and once again . . . nothing should be made which does not give pleasure to the maker and the user, and that pleasure of making must produce art in the hands of the workman.[12]

Only when the class system is abolished will the beautiful handmade object be once again the norm, but at the same time, the presence of beautiful handmade objects will help bring about this desired end, for Morris believed that encounters with beautiful objects create longings for more such encounters, igniting the intense desires necessary to motivate revolution.[13]

And thus Morris, like Niedecker, ties class struggle and exploitation directly to war and violence, seeing the former as an example of the latter. One response to this violence (one *immediate* response, that is, because after reading Marx in 1881, Morris firmly believed in the eventual abolishment of the class system) lies in experiencing, as producer and consumer, the handmade and freely circulating object.[14] Elizabeth Willis describes a similar vision in Niedecker: "Niedecker clearly saw the abjection of the poet within American culture, but she also saw it countered by the dizzying freedom of working with others almost entirely beyond the bounds of the market economy, in the realm of barter and free exchange."[15] Niedecker's poem "His Carpets Flowered," which draws much of its material from Morris's letters, illustrates these shared ideals, as it moves between descriptions of crafting ("I designed a carpet today"; "to get done / the work of the hand"; "Good sport dyeing / tapestry wool") to political critique ("now that the gall / of our society's // corruption stains throughout"). For both writers, then, the handcrafted object (and the poem as an example of such) becomes a mark of resistance to the violence of labor and class under capitalism.

Niedecker wrote *NEXT YEAR OR I FLY MY ROUNDS, TEMPESTUOUS* on scraps of paper, which she then glued to the pages of a pocket calendar from 1935, pasting her poems directly over the homilies the calendar originally displayed. The resulting poem, perhaps more than anything else, is about time—specifically, as Elizabeth Robinson has noted,[16] it's about two temporalities in competition with one another. The first, materially represented by the calendar itself, is ordinary chronological time—clock time, countable, progressive, linear time, maybe factory time; the second, announced first by the poem's title, is circular or cyclical time—the temporality of the natural world, or of the poet who sees herself as contiguous with that world, and perhaps also the temporality embraced by lovers who resist the normative narrative of romantic relationships.[17] This alternate, resistant temporality (resistant not just to calendar time itself but also, one could say, to all the institutions that rely on its predictability and regularity) replaces the squares by which the calendar counts its days with "rounds," which the speaker "flies," as a bird flies her rounds gathering fragments and scraps for her nest.

Thus Niedecker establishes her claim on nonlinear time simply through repurposing and retitling the calendar. She makes it even more explicit in the opening poem, which reads in its entirety: "Wade all life / backward to its / source which / runs too far / ahead." Life is figured as a fantastical river, an endlessly looping fluidity with a source both before and behind us. To "wade" through life, one must enter this looping rather than progressive movement, one must "revolve," as the next poem tells us.[18] "The satisfactory / emphasis is on / revolving" begins that poem, and then Niedecker introduces what I see as the poem's secondary but related theme: romantic love. "Don't send / steadily: after / you know me / I'll be no one," the poem concludes. Reading this as advice to the lover (and admittedly, there are other ways to read it), one might paraphrase: "Don't send for me, don't pursue me, because as soon as you think you 'know' me, I'll simply dissolve, becoming no one." But is this a statement of anxiety or a claim for autonomous identity?

As Rachel Blau DuPlessis has argued, to be "no one," to exist in relative anonymity, was for Niedecker a political choice. With anonymity comes a deep connection to the "folk," to the collective, and to art as the voice of this collective. With anonymity too comes a way to preserve integrity, for it's a form of withholding, of resisting full participation in a world whose values one does not share.

> Scuttle up the workshop,
> settle down the dew,
> I'll tell you what my name is
> when we've made the world anew

wrote Niedecker just a few years later. "Her anonymity," claims DuPlessis, "is then a utopian gamble; she'll have a name when social and political changes begin to transform the class and gender materials which she spent a lifetime analyzing."[19] If we accept this argument (and I find it convincing), we might then read the end of this fragile and ambiguous second poem of I FLY MY ROUNDS less as an attempt to protect identity or selfhood and more as a claim to the freedoms of anonymity. To extend this just a bit, I'd say that the claim to anonymity is also a way to resist the particular violence that normative kinship identifications might entail.

The poems that follow continue to circle, or "revolve," around Eros—referencing the "heat" that bodies give off, females with flowers, a man holding a woman's knees, monogamy, bathroom luxuries, the endearments "darling" and "my love." And then, toward the end of the sequence, perhaps with tongue in cheek, Niedecker references one of our culture's foundational romantic scenes, thereby introducing the violence that is perhaps lurking behind these poems all along:

> Balcony scene in
> Romeo and Juliet—
> a white kerchief
> comes into a

pocket shirred
onto a blue silk
gown.

Or from Row
L in the balcony?

Focusing on just the final two lines of this poem (though much could be said about the variously arranged objects in lines 3–7), we find interesting confusions. Elizabeth Robinson notes that "from Row / L in the balcony" positions the speaker (or someone) in the audience, perhaps watching *Romeo and Juliet* unfold.[20] This is convincing, but given that "Row" could easily be short for "Romeo," there are other ways to read these lines as well. Perhaps they wonder whether the kerchief (the only noun that could readily take the place of direct object here) has been dropped *from* the balcony above, but in that case "Row" would be in the balcony rather than in the courtyard as we expect him to be. If "L" is an initial (rather than a row designation), then we begin to wonder if "L" stands for Lorine, in which case Lorine is "in the balcony," standing in for Juliet. But "L" could as easily stand for Louis, the lover to whom so many of these poems are addressed. This leaves us nowhere, or more readily, anywhere. "L" could be a row name, or it could be Row's name. Either L, Lorine or Louis, could be in the balcony; either could be below.

It does seem that Niedecker is playing with the lovers' shared initial here, for "What's in a name?" as Juliet says. If "I'll be no one," why must I bear a name at all ("Romeo, doff thy name")? Indeed, the violence of belonging to a name, the violence that clinging to kinship can generate, is Shakespeare's theme: "'Tis but thy name that is my enemy"; "The orchard walls are high and hard to climb, / And the place death, considering who thou art, / If any of my kinsmen find thee here."[21] The play's true battle is not between Montagues and Capulets but between the enforced boundaries of family, name, and property and the freedom and anonymity of erotic love and desire. Reading back now to the second poem discussed above, perhaps we can understand better the stakes in being "no one." To be no one is to resist the violence of kinship pacts, of names, property and patriarchal family.[22] That *I FLY MY ROUNDS,* despite its surrealist tendencies, is in some way a poem of protest becomes even clearer when Niedecker writes, "I don't hum / the least of my resistance, / I give it fly."[23]

Indeed flight is a recurring metaphor in these poems, as it is in Shakespeare's play, signaling in both works the liberty of love against the rigidity and violence of the patriarchal family. Recall that when Juliet asks Romeo how he arrived in the Capulets' orchard he answers, "With love's light wings did I o'er-perch these walls; / For stony limits cannot hold love out, / And what love can do that dares love attempt; / Therefore thy kinsmen are no let to me."[24] This rejection of walls is echoed throughout Niedecker's poem too, perhaps most simply in the final poem in which she writes, "Jesus, I'm / going out / and throw / my arms / around." "I would I were thy bird," says Romeo to Juliet; says Niedecker to Zukofsky: "I like a / loved one to / be apt in / the wing." The small, intimate gesture—the gift, be it the poem or the ring that Juliet passes to Romeo—is also birdlike, a frail and free thing, momentarily escaping, even as it points to, the violence of the surrounding culture.

Thirty years later, as Lyndon Johnson waged all-out war in Vietnam, Niedecker created her *Homemade Poems* for Cid Corman. (Thanks to the Lost and Found project at CUNY, directed by Ammiel Alcalay, *Homemade Poems* is now available in a facsimile edition.) Along with this gift, she included the following letter:

Dear Cid,

I somehow feel compelled to send you the product of the last year, just to keep in touch. I know you're not printing [*Origin*]. I even brave school kid's paints to show where we live! It's been ____ *a year!* I wish you and Louie and Celia and I could sit around a table. Otherwise, poetry has to do it.

Please don't mind my 'metaphysical' in my last letter. I meant it but evidently didn't use the right word. Your work and Louie's, there's no use—for me—to look farther.

These then with love—
Lorine[25]

The poems stand in for the physical proximity of one's friends. They are made with love, with love in mind, on a small pad bound with cardboard and covered in wrapping paper, which includes a watercolor by Niedecker of her house on Black Hawk Island. Much less obscure than the poems of *I FLY MY ROUNDS,* these handwritten lyrics discuss love and friendship directly, such as in "Laundromat": "Casual, sudsy // social love // at the tubs," and the following untitled poem: "If only my friend / would return / and remove the leaves / from my eaves / troughs." There are poems for or about Ian Finlay, Zukofsky, and Niedecker's husband, Albert Millen ("He's / the one for me"), about important nineteenth-century radicals, Margaret Fuller, Mary Shelley, and Ruskin, and about weather and the seasons. A gesture of friendship and a poetics, the book opens in the midst of debate: "Consider at the outset: / to be thin for thought / or thick cream blossomy." Corman's work, which Niedecker loved ("Sun Rock Man is so *good,*" she exclaims in `63),[26] is famous for being "thin" on the page. Comparable to Robert Creeley's narrow verses, his poems are dense, nonetheless, with thought. Niedecker ends this poem with a teasing admonishment—"don't be afraid / to pour wine over cabbage"—but from this moment of play, she deepens the terms of friendship: "Ah your face / but it's whether / you can keep me warm." Here, in just three lines, we discover the vulnerabilities, the differences, the need, and the doubt that real friendships encompass.

References to war and violence are here too, more overtly than in *I FLY MY ROUNDS:*

Spring
  stood there
    all body

Head
  blown off
    (war)

showed up
  downstream

October
        in the head
            of spring

Birch, sumac
    before
        the blast

Spring is a headless body, its head floating downstream with October inside: a surreal image for sure, but not inexplicable. On the one hand, it speaks of springtime's ability to blast us out of thought into sensation, which is the theme of another poem a few pages later in which Niedecker writes, "As you know mind / aint what attracts me / . . . but what was sensed / by them guys." On the other hand, the poem points away from the immediacy and pleasures of spring to something much darker, for by 1963 blown off heads and other gore are starting to show up in the news. With war in mind and in memory, the birch and sumac at the end of the poem take on a nostalgic feel, as if the poem longs for a previous time of peace and pleasure, a time "before the blast."

And yet, a yearning toward the sensual is itself not at all trivial. It is, I think, what ties all the poems in this volume together. It's the dare with which the book opens ("don't be afraid to pour wine over cabbage") and with which it ends. "Wild strawberries," the final poem begins, "Ruskin's consolation // His grey diaries / instanced with Rose." The pleasures of body, tongue, and nose, of the meal with friends she imagines in her accompanying letter—it's the work of poetry to remind us of these things, to take us out of our heads, the "Metaphysical Club," and return us to the body with its longings, pleasures, vulnerabilities, and loves. And, of course, the handmade book is not only an immediate vehicle for these ideas, it's also an instantiation of them. Bearing the mark of the hand, it becomes an emissary of the body, an instance of what Niedecker calls "Life's dance," in which "social love" draws us near.

How this "labor of love" functions in opposition to violence and war becomes evident four months later. In February of `65 Niedecker writes to Corman again, this time proposing an anthology of short poems, "just the essence of poetry," in which she imagines including two of Sappho's poems, translated by Mary Barnard. The second of these I quote in full:

> Some say a cavalry corps,
> some infantry, some again,
> will maintain that the swift ones
> of our fleet are the finest
> sight on dark earth; but I say
> that whatever one loves, is.[27]

The poem speaks for itself, but one item deserves to be pointed out, and that is the comma in the final line. I don't know how Barnard justified this comma, knowing nothing of Sappho's Greek, but in English the choice is striking. The pause allows the poem's obvious assertion (that the finest sight on earth, rather than being the institutions and tools of war, is whatever one loves) to open into a far more radical claim: that love is generative, that if we love something we bring it *thereby* into being. Certainly this is true of poetry, for poets anyway. But it's also true of friendship—a "thing" that doesn't exist without our love. And it's this belief that abides in the handmade object and that allows these fragile, seemingly ephemeral things to function as instances of resistance to love's opponents: violence and war.

I would now like to turn briefly to three poet-artists from our time: Linda Norton, Jill Magi, and Maria Damon. My desire to write about some of the work by these women has less to do with their being directly influenced by Niedecker (though with Norton, that is certainly the case)[28] than with the specific qualities of their work. For each of these women, the handmade poem/object is in direct response to war—specifically to the wars on terror we are now, and seemingly forevermore, engaged in. More broadly understood, their works are a response to violence in its many forms and institutions. I will begin with Norton, focusing not on her writing here (though it also engages questions of violence, especially in relation to poverty and race) but on her collage work, for it's in this discipline that I find her closest to Niedecker.

Fig. 2. Linda Norton, from "Dark White," 2014.

In a series of collages she titled "Dark White," images of World War II and Vietnam soldiers, taken from a water-logged book on the history of photography and a guide to Vietnam collectibles, are positioned in diagonal relationship to images of mostly domestic objects, clipped from magazines. In one case a large cooking pot hangs over the head of a solider seated cross-legged on the ground eating a meal. In another, an open drawer containing folded clothes or linens hovers near a soldier's helmeted head. A third shows three soldiers bent over, stalking with rifles out, while above their bent backs, a bath towel, or perhaps the corner of a sheet, seems to hang suspended.

That these modest collages are works of protest seems to me obvious, but exactly what they protest is not so easy to say. On the one hand, we might see the domestic objects as providing the soldiers with some kind of comfort, as if existing in their dreams or as if signaling homes and families that await them. On the other hand, Norton, very much like Niedecker, is acutely aware of the close relationship between war and capitalism. These commodities, then, far from being the antidote to war and its discomforts, are in fact its motive-cause. They hover above the heads of these soldiers less like angels and more like dictating gods—threatening and demanded, pressing the soldiers into action. These contrasting readings are what make the collages so haunting and what make them most like Neidecker's poems too, for Niedecker also holds a very ambivalent relationship to domestic space, at once valuing its privacy and quiet and, at the same time, reviling the ownership and commodification that domestic space tends to insist upon.[29]

Jill Magi, like Norton, works in a variety of disciplines: poetry, prose, bookmaking, embroidery, and other textile work. Her website's list of works includes "Book Works," "Stitched Works," "Remnants," "Threads," and "Small Books." Her works range from large-scale installation and durational performance to ephemeral and immediate objects (under the category "Small Books" Magi has written: "Written quickly, typed up, stapled, and given away"). Her newest book, a work of fiction titled *LABOR*, explores the hierarchization of academic labor—contrasting the lives of characters (an archivist, an activist, an adjunct professor, and a tenured professor) engaged in various levels of institutional labor. *LABOR* has another life too, as a performance/installation. Describing the making of this version of *LABOR*, Magi writes,

> *LABOR* began with my virtual, screen-based encounter with the Wagner Labor Archive finding guide. At that time, in 2008, it was all on-line. On election-day, while some felt hopeful about Obama and "change," I felt depressed and became engrossed with entry after entry of "radical" US history and labor activism. Electronically, I highlighted, copied, and pasted the entire finding guide, chunk by chunk, into a word document, printed it out and slapped a title page on it: *LABOR*. But I knew I needed to mediate the language. So I went to the archive itself, and called up random files so that I could just sit there and touch the pages. I didn't know what I would do with any of it. Before the book came out, I took this printed-out finding guide and attempted to recopy all of its entries by hand on large sheets of newsprint. I filmed this. I only got about 10% in. My hand was cramping and the work was excruciating—I also had a sequence of nightmares featuring dead people who were very unhappy. I had to stop.[30]

Clearly Magi's work addresses the problems of commodity culture and labor inequities in a variety of strategies involving the handmade. Here I would like to focus on her 2011 book *SLOT*. *SLOT* turns to the memorial, especially the war memorial, as a failed site of public grieving and accountability. Poems draw text from the websites and pamphlets of public memorials, often war memorials, but also civil rights memorials, and others. We are given a sense of the futility or presumption of these sites in passages such as the following:

Dear Theater:

By climbing aboard the actual bus on which Rosa Parks' protest began, we can sit down and become the subject to a recording of the driver's voice demanding that we, positioned as Rosa Parks, move or leave.

. . .

Hall of Commitment:

Here they sign a statement of personal commitment to the cause, their portrait is taken and their faces are added to a video-mosaic of faces that merge and rise up the tower in an iconic representation of the community of Human Rights constantly replenishing itself.[31]

Or in the following perverse instance:

At the Colonial Williamsburg Escaped Slave Program, began in 2000, guests are approached by a runaway slave. Visitors know that they are surrounded by slave catchers and so the park's guests must react instinctively to the situation. "This has turned out to be a really intense visitor experience and is one of its most popular programs."[32]

A few pages later Magi highlights the distancing effect of the war memorial in particular: "In the elevator, a recording of a soldier's voice describes the scene and concludes by asking: "'How could it happen?' / Purchase a guidebook. Walk through the notorious gate."[33] The memorial-as-spectacle becomes in these pages yet another form of violence as it grants its visitors a false sense of empathy, or an easily earned (the price of a ticket) representation of their own participation in the "community of Human Rights," offering them a "way out"—a way to avoid, rather than answer, the soldier's fundamental question.

But *SLOT* also includes photographs, and it's in these images that Magi seems to suggest alternate forms of engagement. One series of images shows us Magi's own hands, engaged in some sort of struggle with knotted thread. During the time she was writing *SLOT* Magi was also working on an installation she called "Wall Piece" in which she pierced her studio's walls with hundreds of tiny holes into which she glued strings. She then "played" the strings like a harp, producing a tangled mess of knots. In this series of images her hands are shown tangling and untangling these knots, as if indicating the complexity of the problems that her text explores. Magi also includes photographs of her hands holding swatches of cloth over the museum maps and brochures. In this sequence, the gentle touch of the hand suggests a covering, as one might cover a baby, or a shrouding, as one might shroud the dead. The brochures have been speaking to us all along with their institutional voice, their failed attempts to heal. In these sets of images the hand interrupts with its own language—a language of struggle and difficulty, a language of touch and intimacy and care.

By way of conclusion I'll turn finally to the needlepoint poetry of poet, textile artist, and critic Maria Damon.[34] Most of Damon's handmade works are at least originally gifts for friends, such as the piece titled "Mark's Now," made for her friend the poet Mark Nowak when he "came out as a Marxist," which simply displays the word "Red," or the piece titled "EM" in memory of Emma Bernstein, made as a gift to her parents and brother, in which a highly decorative "E" is surrounded by the names of the family members. The piece I would like to discuss here is titled "Dreams I and II." It includes two rectangular cloths embroidered with the word "Poetry" in elaborate font and multiple colors.[35] In a short introduction to this work Damon explains that the project arose after her friend Stephen Vincent posted a comment about a dream on a poetry listserv: "Quite literally I had a dream last night in which the garment industry in league with the poets in opposition to the advent of war started sewing 'poetry' tags on to pants, shirts, blouses, etc. Similar to the old— or maybe it still goes on—little red Levi's tag on jeans," Vincent wrote in February 2003 as the War on Terror entered its second year. "I won't spend my Sunday morning," he continues, "deducing all the implications, possibilities, down or upsides of a populace whether domestically, in school work or on the street with 'poetry' as both an intimate and public banner—with 'peace' or 'anti-war gesture' by implication."[36]

Of course, this is just a quick note, casually posted, not a carefully worked-through statement, but what I find most interesting and most moving is the assumption Vincent lets slide (even as he claims to skirt it)—that "peace" or "anti-war gesture" would be implied by the simple word "poetry." Evidently, Damon found it moving too, for she carried his dream into material presence. Obviously, a gesture like this can do nothing to impede a war. But poetry is almost always an intimate gesture, and it effects change at the level of the individual. The implications of "Dreams I and II"—a work that includes Vincent's dream, his communication of the dream, the reception of the dream, the sewing and photographing of the pieces, and the free publication of the pieces as part of Damon's online book *Meshwards*—is that poetry matters in the face of war. It matters not because it will save lives (though it can in other ways) but because it is a labor of love, a labor for love—and as such, it stands against war and all the institutions that support war. And perhaps when the hand of the maker is most evident, felt in the very fibers of the object, the intimacy and urgency of the labor are all the more potent.

And so I end this essay where I began, in a dream, the dream in which love counters war. It's a vital dream, a necessary dream, but it will inevitably feel futile, even despairing, to its dreamers. Let me return, then, to William Morris. In the final passage of *News from Nowhere,* his protagonist, William Guest, having concluded his visit to the utopian future, is awakening in present-day London:

I lay in my bed in my house at dingy Hammersmith thinking about it all; and trying to consider if I was overwhelmed with

Fig 3. Maria Damon, "Dream 1," 2002.

despair at finding I had been dreaming a dream; and strange to say, I found that I was not so despairing.

Or indeed was it a dream? If so, why was I so conscious all along that I was really seeing all that new life from the outside, still wrapped up in the prejudices, the anxieties, the distrust of this time of doubt and struggle?

All along, though those friends were so real to me, I had been feeling as if I had no business amongst them: as though the time would come when they would reject me, and say, as Ellen's last mournful look seemed to say, "No, it will not do; you cannot be of us; you belong so entirely to the unhappiness of the past that our happiness even would weary you. Go back again, now you have seen us, and your outward eyes have learned that in spite of all the infallible maxims of your day there is yet a time of rest in store for the world, when mastery has changed into fellowship—but not before. Go back again, then, and while you live you will see all round you people engaged in making others live lives which are not their own, while they themselves care nothing for their own real lives—men who hate life though they fear death. Go back and be the happier for having seen us, for having added a little hope to your struggle. Go on living while you may, striving, with whatsoever pain and labour needs must be, to build up little by little the new day of fellowship, and rest, and happiness."

Yes, surely! and if others can see it as I have seen it, then it may be called a vision rather than a dream.[37]

Notes

1. Margaret Ronda, "*Disenchanted Georgics: The Aesthetics of Labor in American Poetry*" (PhD diss., University of California Berkeley, 2009).

2. Eleni Sikelianos, "Life Pops from a Music Box Shaped Like a Gun: Dismemberments and Mendings in Niedecker's Figures," in *Radical Vernacular: Lorine Niedecker and the Poetics of Place*, ed. Elizabeth Willis (Iowa City: University of Iowa Press, 2008), 31. As formal choices are always also political and affective choices, one way to understand the constructivist archival drive in the Modernist long or serial poem in general (Williams, H.D., Olson, Oppen) is as this healing work of salvage.

3. Elizabeth Willis, "The Poetics of Affinity: Niedecker, Morris, and the Art of Work," in *Radical Vernacular*, ed. Willis, 223.

4. Lorine Niedecker, *Collected Works*, ed. Jenny Penberthy (Berkeley: University of California Press, 2002), 95, 165, 170, 137.

5. See Kirsty Robertson, "Rebellious Doilies and Subversive Stitches: Writing and Craftivist History," and Anthea Black and Nicole Burisch, "Craft Hard Die Free: Radical Curatorial Strategies for Craftivism," in *Extra/Ordinary: Craft and Contemporary Art,* ed. Maria Buszek (Durham, NC: Duke University Press, 2011), 184–203, 204–21. These essays and others in the volume detail craftivism's history of protest, especially against nuclear arms in the 1980s and the World Trade Organization in the early 2000s.

6. Robertson, "Rebellious Doilies," 187.

7. Anne Cvetkovich, *Depression: A Public Feeling* (Durham, NC: Duke University Press, 2012), 168.

8. Robertson, "Rebellious Doilies," 195–96.

9. Ibid., 185.

10. These activities are not without their detractors—often feminists themselves—who see the work of "craftivism" as a regressive return to homey comforts or as futile forms of pretest. See Robertson, "Rebellious Doilies," 191.

11. Willis, "Poetics of Affinity," 229.

12. William Morris, "Art Under Plutocracy," The William Morris Internet Archive, accessed May 25, 2017, https://www.marxists.org/archive/morris/works/index.htm.

13. Carr, *Surface Tension,* 147–88, 182–83.

14. Morris clearly articulates his vision for a post-capitalist society, in which handcrafted objects circulate freely, in his utopian novel, *News from Nowhere.* In reality, his design company, "The Firm," to Morris's own consternation, produced finely made home furnishings for the

rich. See Fiona MacCarthy, *William Morris: A Life for Our Time* (New York: Knopf, 1995), 210.

15. Willis, "Poetics of Affinity," 226.

16. Elizabeth Robinson, "Music Becomes Story: Lyric and Narrative Patterning in the Work of Lorine Niedecker," in Willis, *Radical Vernacular*, 188–124.

17. Niedecker sent the calendar book to Zukofsky during the period of their most intense romantic interaction. "Given that the poem was held by Zukofsky and given his dating on the back of the calendar—'Xmas 1934'—the poem was likely Niedecker's gift to the poet whom she had now known in person for a full calendar year. The gift looks forward confidently to another year of friendship just as it recalls the past year. A pocket calendar, an intimate mnemonics. But the poem is also a surrealist composition and an experiment in form. The calendar itself is under siege." Jenny Penberthy, "Editor's Note," *Sulfur* 41 (Fall 1997), accessed May 26, 2017, http://epc.buffalo.edu/authors/niedecker/calendar.html.

18. Another, though oblique, reference to this resistant temporality occurs some pages later. In the poem for May 19–June 1, Niedecker references Salvador Dali's painting "Archeological Reminiscence of Millet's Angelus." Surrealism was important to Niedecker at that time (and a point of contention between she and Zukofsky, who was less enthralled), but perhaps Dali is particularly important because of his melting watches, which emblematize a refusal of linear time. The painting referenced is itself a blending or melting of temporalities, for Dali repaints Jean-François Millet's *L'Angelus,* transforming Millet's farmworkers into semi-abstracted sculptural forms.

19. Rachel Blau DuPlessis, "Lorine Niedecker, the Anonymous: Gender, Class, Genre and Resistances," in *Lorine Niedecker: Woman and Poet,* ed. Jenny Penberthy (Orono, ME: National Poetry Foundation, 1996), 137.

20. Robinson, "Music Becomes Story," 124.

21. William Shakespeare, *Romeo and Juliet,* II.2:859–62, accessed May 25, 2017, http://shakespeare.mit.edu/romeo_juliet/full.html.

22. Perhaps it's too much of a stretch to read these delicate, ambiguous poems as responding to the rise of fascism, but I can't help thinking that a critique of boundaries, walls, and kinship ties comes to bear on world history as it was unfolding in the mid-1930s.

23. Robinson reads this line as suggesting a letting go of resistance rather than a soaring (or increase) of (political) resistance. I concur that it could be read either way. Robinson, "Music Becomes Story," 122.

24. Shakespeare, *Romeo and Juliet,* II.2:864–67.

25. Lisa Pater Faranda, ed., *"Between Your House and Mine": The Letters of Lorine Niedecker and Cid Corman, 1960–1970* (Durham, NC: Duke University Press, 1986), 48.

26. Ibid., 35.

27. Ibid., 51–52.

28. As Norton explains: "My Niedecker story starts with working at Inland Book Company in 1985, and finding a copy of Cid Corman's *ORIGIN* with her work in it. I still have it. Inland Book Company was like the SPD [Small Press Distribution] of the East Coast. It was in East Haven, CT, a bus ride and a world away from Yale. It was on an ugly stretch of road where the sycamores were all weirdly amputated. Nearby: a mattress factory and a cheese factory. I would wait for the bus back to Yale with workers from those factories. Most were developmentally disabled. Some smelled like cheese. Among the folk, like Niedecker. Then much later when I moved to Berkeley [to be the poetry editor at the University of California Press] I went down to SPD and bought the Jargon Society volume. Working and working to get the book [Niedecker's *Collected Works*] under contract, talking with Jenny Penberthy, leaving [the job] a little before it was published, getting it in the mail, being very HAPPY. Somewhere in there, I was so broke, I sold all my Jargon Society editions to Moe's. No regrets." Private email, November 3, 2014.

29. As noted in *"Between Your House and Mine,"* in her later years Niedecker selected domestic and private life over a more overt politically or socially active life. As she wrote in a note to Bob Nero, rejecting his invitation to dinner, "I don't mourn the lone-ness of it [her life] for poetry. In fact . . . I have the presumption to feel that others writing should retire into themselves deeper than they do." Faranda, 84–85. As an instance of Niedecker's critique of private property, and there are many, we have the following poem, titled "Foreclosure": "Tell em to take my bare walls down / my cement abutments / their parties thereof / and clause of claws // Leave me the land / Scratch out: the land // May prose and property both die out / and leave me peace." Significantly for this essay, it seems "poetry" (not prose) more readily aligns with peace. *Collected Works*, 291.

30. Private email, November 8, 2014. This handmade-work failure is documented in Yelena Gluzman and Sophia Cleary, eds., *Emergency Index: Vol. 2* (New York: Ugly Duckling Presse, 2012).

31. Jill Magi, *SLOT* (New York: Ugly Duckling Presse, 2011), 33.

32. Ibid., 44.

33. Ibid., 57.

34. Damon is the author of *Postliterary America: From Bagel Shop Jazz to Micropoetries* (University of Iowa Press, 2011) and *The Dark End of the*

Street: Margins in American Vanguard Poetry (University of Minnesota Press, 1993), among other works. In these books she explores the poetry of marginalized subcultures and nontraditional or extra-literary spaces and communities.

35. Images of these and the other pieces have been published as a free pdf titled *Meshwards* by Dusie Press, http://www.dusie.org/Damon%20 Meshwards.pdf.

36. Stephen Vincent, Buffalo Poetics listserv, February 23, 2003, accessed November 12, 2014, https://listserv.buffalo.edu/cgi-bin/ wa?HOME.

37. William Morris, *News from Nowhere*, The William Morris Internet Archive, accessed November 12, 2014, https://www.marxists.org/ar chive/morris/works/index.htm.

Ralph Lemon, Fred Moten, and the Unspeakable

An Improvisatory Line

I've been reading Fred Moten for only five years. That's not that long, but it might also be true that I've *only* been reading Fred Moten for five years, in that few other writers have kept me reading, hanging, suspended right where I want to be, which is at the edge, at "the little edges"—at the edge of understanding but refusing understanding, because everything I understand Fred to say rejects or revises "understanding" in the ways I've understood it to mean.

And so I'm thinking about Moten and the unspeakable not from the position of one who understands and can explicate, unpack, or describe Moten, as if you have not also been reading Moten and better and longer than I have. Instead, what I want to focus on is one relationship in Moten's work, one moment of contact that is also, I believe, an improvisation, and so, one moment of contact improvisation.

Still, I think it might not be hyperbolic to say that Fred Moten is the philosopher of our time. As the philosopher of blackness, of being and of nothingness, of the social, of the common and the undercommon, he guides readers and listeners through language that suspends right at the lip of the poetic cliff, language that opens toward new ways of being together in the world.

"I believe in the world and I want to be in it. I want to be in it all the way to the end of it because I believe in another world in the world and I want to be in *that.*" (Moten, spoken comment)

So how to do we enter this work or this world? There are many ways in, and there are no easy ways.

Here is one:

Fig. 4. Ralph Lemon's *Come Home Charlie Patton*. Photo by R. Eric Stone.

Near the end of "the Proscenium portion" of choreographer/
artist/writer Ralph Lemon's multimedia work "Come Home
Charlie Patton," Lemon stands inside a wooden box, his pro-
file to the audience, speaking into a mike. The story he tells (a
mash-up of his own writing, that of Arne Bontemps, and histori-
cal documentation of the (in)famous 1921 lynching in Duluth,
Minnesota) is of Elias, who, as a child, watches two people (one
is his grandmother) ride a horse off a cliff. This calm and sur-
real suicide or escape, this moment of falling, which is also re-
lease, becomes part and parcel of Elias's "trouble." Years later,
Lemon narrates, he is arrested on his birthday, seized just at the
date of his becoming, so that he becomes altered or enters an
altered becoming. On his return home, says Lemon, "he makes
this dance."

And what is this dance?

Lemon leaves the box and enters a stage (a stage on a stage).
There he begins a soft shoe, a shuffle, a slip and fall, the so-
called buck dance: head down, body a little curved inward. And
then another dancer emerges, dragging with him a long and
large-mouthed fire hose. The water's on, the dance too, under,
within, and against the hard-hitting hose. Of course he falls,
over and over, and once he's down another appears, dancing
downstage, then a third who learns his steps from the woman
in front. Eventually Charlie Patton, who's been singing through
the speakers, turns punk, the buck dance too, punk. Eventually
the dancers dance so hard they hit the floor. And then, the si-
rens come, and lights too, hard headlights of the law.
    I want to think about the relationship, then, between the law
and the dance, between the arrest and the fall, in terms I'll bor-
row from Moten.
    Moten has written of Lemon in a poem he calls "Hard enough
to enjoy."

> Charged with the blackness of physics its extralegal social
>   surrealities, in
>   search of

conceptual thaw having survived the river's violent floes and
    squalls, its
    seizing distancing, but drawn to the river of rivers of
        rivers, Lemon began a long series of residencies in
        itinerance.[1]

Itinerance, or what Moten calls elsewhere and often "fugitiv-
ity," *is* the "extralegal social surreality" of blackness, *extra*legal
because, as Moten discusses in the essays "Knowledge and Free-
dom," "Blackness and Governance," and elsewhere, blackness
neither precedes nor follows the law and is at once outside of
and within it. I'll return, but let me turn now to an echo I find
here.

The "river of rivers of rivers" that Moten says Lemon is drawn
to, if it is a reference to Wallace Stevens's "The River of Rivers
in Connecticut," wouldn't be the first time that Stevens makes a
presence in Moten's writing (see "Blackness and Nothingness,"
which is in some part a long riff on "The Snowman"). In Ste-
vens's poem[2] the great river runs—a gayety, reflecting steeple
and town, headed "nowhere, like the sea." Flowing (like so much
in Stevens) from fact to myth, or thing to no-thing, the river is
forceful, a "vigor," but then conceptual, an "abstraction" (much
like the law). It is, Stevens tells us, only discernable by way of
what it reflects: "It is not to be seen beneath the appearances //
That tell of it." Tied, then, to Stevens's other late poems about
the mind, the poem troubles imminence, turning and turning
away from the object it announces.

It's not so easy to decide, in Stevens, whether things ever re-
ally exist, whether the voice of the real is anything more than the
"scrawny cry" of the chorister who precedes the choir, or wheth-
er even that timid note is only a "sound in the mind" ("Not Ideas
about the Thing but the Thing Itself").

But Moten messes with Stevens's ear for nothingness, for the
river in Moten's poem is definitely not Stevens's unnamed force-
ful curricular Connecticut (a trope of whiteness if ever there was
one). In Moten's "river of river of rivers," that third "river" acts
like a double (or triple?) negative, putting a spin on the mind
and turning it around again to face the real.

"River of river of rivers": I feel like a child saying this, and that's right. Because a babbling river, or a babbling word, gets closer to the "nonsense" that Fred names "fugitive presence"— the here and not here of the body that hovers between (or un- divides) mind and matter, between "the lawlessness of the imagi- nation" and the bound flesh of historical presence.

It feels right to babble[3] too because the dancer is like the child, living always between "real life" and the whispered free space of the imagination. As the great "an-original" Contact Im- proviser Steve Paxton liked to say, "Physicists know space, poets know point of view; dancers know both."[4]

The dancer, put perhaps more directly, cannot escape the body even if playing in the mind. The dancer cannot and does not want to escape what it knows of his placement in history and in law, within nation and family, under the lights, through the air, and in the water of real-time present-day violence and real- time present-day pleasure. "Hard enough to enjoy."

"Dancing is what we make of falling. Music is what we make of music's absence, the real presence making music underneath. I'm exhausted so my soul is rested." ("Hard enough to enjoy")

In the essay "Knowledge and Freedom" Moten begins with a mo- ment in Kant's third Critique in which Kant acknowledges the "lawless freedom" of the imagination as that which requires tem- pering, or policing, by the "lawfullness of the understanding." Without understanding's laws, the imagination, says Kant, will produce only nonsense.

Moten runs in right there—into that dynamic between law and imagination—as a kind of rupture or rapture in the discipline—runs into what he calls "an irregular opening of the regulative." "The understanding," he writes, "in its unexplained and unattainable completeness, having been invoked as that which polices the imagination in its lawlessness, is itself both constituted and restrained by imaginative excess."[5] Hegelian so often, Moten reminds—there is no law without lawlessness, no understanding without imagination's escape from it.

Moten ties, and finds Kant tying, this lawless imagination, this "freedom," to blackness, even more to female blackness, which he turns toward as a trope of resistance.

I want to consider this necessarily irregular opening of the regulative and to think it in relation to Kant's deployment of race as the exemplary regulative and/or teleological principle. . . . Thus my interest in the resistance to "[t]his politics of curtailment" that Kant prescribes. Such resistance, which might be called a radical politics of the imagination . . . is here and now inseparable from the racialization and sexualization—at once phantasmatic and experiential—of the imagination.[6]

But it would be too simple to find in the dance only two opposing features: the hose as law, as whiteness, as governance, as restraint, and the dancer as imagination, as lawlessness, as blackness and as freedom. It would be too simple to say also that law speaks and lawlessness utters nonsense, to map these figures (to borrow from elsewhere) onto Kristeva's symbolic and semiotic, or onto Joan Retallack's intelligibility and silence,[7] for what keeps me on the brink with Moten and with Lemon is the slipping and the falling between such oppositions.

The hose and the unspeakable violence it recalls does not produce the dance as an answer. Because the dance, you'll remember, precedes the hose. As Moten puts it, "What's important, here, is to recognize that the melodramatic imagination is indispensable to the critical philosophy, is the dark invaginative foundation—and the secret, anti-foundational rupture—of its systematicity."[8]

Invagination: that term that evokes nativity also describes a falling or folding in that makes the opposition between outer and inner impossible. To say, then, that the dancer responds to the law with her lawlessness would be as wrong as to say that the law responds to her with its vigor—or as right. The improvisation, the contact improvisation, between the forces of movement, of freedom, and of escape and the forces of stillness, of seizure, and of control—is, in the end, what the dance is, what it speaks.[9]

"Only sheer violence is mute" (Hannah Arendt).[10] But it's when things get unspeakable that the poem, as such, is *most* called for, answering that call not with speech per se but with speech's break, its broken cry. Recognizing that the very structures that we resist are also those that define us, poetic language perverts the fissure in that confrontation, that "irregular opening" between the sound-dance of reckless music and language of and as the law.

Perversion, in a poetic landscape, might look or sound like nonsense. In a dance it might look like falling, like hitting the floor.

In the real world of the law that kills yet faces no law, the real world that precedes and follows "Come Home Charlie Patton" in which the white crowd gathers to cheer the lynching, or floods the floor at the convention of its supremacy, imagination's perversions might look like criminality, its language might sound like a scream.[11]

Dancing is what

we make of falling.
Music is what we make of music's absence. The real presence
    making music
    underneath.

I'm exhausted so my soul is rested.

Notes

1. Fred Moten, *The Little Edges* (Middletown, CT: Wesleyan University Press, 2014), 17.
2. Wallace Stevens, *The Collected Poems* (New York: Vintage, 1990), 533.

There is a great river this side of Stygia
Before one comes to the first black cataracts
And trees that lack the intelligence of trees.
In that river, far this side of Stygia,
The mere flowing of the water is a gayety,
Flashing and flashing in the sun. On its banks,
No shadow walks. The river is fateful,
Like the last one. But there is no ferryman.

He could not bend against its propelling force.
It is not to be seen beneath the appearances
That tell of it. The steeple at Farmington
Stands glistening and Haddam shines and sways.
It is the third commonness with light and air,
A curriculum, a vigor, a local abstraction . . .
Call it, one more, a river, an unnamed flowing,
Space-filled, reflecting the seasons, the folk-lore
Of each of the senses; call it, again and again,
The river that flows nowhere, like a sea.

3. "Babble and gobbledygook, *le petit nègre*, the little nigger, pidgin, baby talk, bird talk, Bird's talk, bard talk, bar talk, our locomotive bar walk and black chant, our pallet cries and shipped whispers, our black notes and black cant, the tenor's irruptive habitation of the vehicle, the monastic preparation of a more than three-dimensional transcript" is how Moten describes black speech in "Blackness and Nothingness (Mysticism in the Flesh)," *South Atlantic Quarterly* 112.4 (Fall 2013): 757.

4. Spoken comment, Eden's Expressway, New York City, approximately 1995.

5. Moten, *Stolen Life*.

6. Ibid..

7. "Silence is currently what is audible but unintelligible," writes Joan Retallack, "The realm of the unintelligible is the permanent frontier—that which lies outside the scope of the culturally preconceived—just where we need to operate in our invention of new forms of life." Joan Retallack, *The Poethical Wager* (Berkeley: University of California Press, 2003), 345.

8. Ibid., 38.

9. The concept of what the philosophers call "first principles" or "first postulates" is always breaking down in Moten, who is fond of the term "anoriginal," refusing, in its frequent employment, any origin story for blackness, any origin story for law. First postulates are always breaking down in dance too, at least in Lemon's work. As Lemon's dramaturge, Katherine Profeta, puts it, "Ralph had rejected any 'obvious' display of his research materials on stage as reductive. And we all understood *Patton* as a much larger art process that included a proscenium show, instead of a process leading up to a proscenium goal." One of Profeta's jobs was to write the program notes for *Come Home Charlie Patton*. She describes facing a particularly difficult task: how to narrate a process without seeming to present "research" as preceding and therefore in some sense secondary to the work itself, how to instead present

both research and performance as one. Katherine Profeta, *Dramaturgy in Motion: At Work on Dance and Movement Performance* (Madison: University of Wisconsin Press, 2015), 121.

10. Arendt, *Human Condition,* 26.

11. "I am at the screaming place. . . . I am exhausted. I am repulsed. I am over all the circular dialogue. But I don't know precisely where that leaves me other than in a hurt and festering place," writes *New York Times* columnist Charles Blow in response to the news that no police officers would be convicted for the death of Freddie Gray, despite his death being ruled a homicide by a medical examiner. Charles Blow, "Incandescent with Rage," *New York Times,* July 27, 2016, accessed May 25, 2017, https://www.nytimes.com/2016/07/28/opinion/incandescent-with-rage.html.

On Property and Monstrosity

> If you asked me what God I believed in in political phi-
> losophy, it would have to be the notion that there is no
> such thing as individual freedom, that human freedom is
> finally, always, a project of making a world with others.
> —Wendy Brown[1]

We bought a 1954 gas station surrounded by fruit trees—apple,
pear, peach, plumb, apricot, and cherry—planted a decade ago
by Dan, the previous owner, who, in addition to gardening,
made soccer goals there (Goal Oriented was the name of his
business). Three years ago Dan's wife died and after that, he let
things go. Compass weed (an opiate) and thistle (good for tea)
grew thigh high all around the trees. Volunteer elm sprung up
to compete for light, water, and soil. Berry vines choked tree
trunks, spiraling, twining, and scratching our ankles with their
thorns. All of this had to be cleared, once in the fall and then
again when it all came back in the spring.

There was also a vegetable garden to recreate—beds to clear
(again, the weeds)—raised beds to build, soil and compost to
transport in our little Ford pickup with its broken doors, broken
blinkers, broken window, and broken bed gate, so that we had
to stand in the truck bed shoveling the soil and compost out,
one heavy shovelful at a time. There was planting to do—some
things went in too early, others maybe too late—an irrigation
system had to be created and then, when the dog got to it, re-
paired. The strawberry patch weeded and then, when the birds
ate the berries, netted. Rose vines, mostly dead wood, grew up
and into and around the chain-link that surrounded the garden,
and for many days, weeks really, we cut away the dead wood and

tied up the vines to the fence again where, miraculously in June, they all bloomed—tight little red ones, outrageous orange, flimsy white, baby pink, sexy pink, and even creamy yellow. Finally, after all this, with everything coming up, we turned to the area outside the fence.

Two great big apple trees grew from what could have been the sidewalk, but that there was no walk, only weeds and the trees. Russian sage, mint, compass weed, various grasses and dandelion. The trees hadn't been pruned for so long they were almost unrecognizable as apples, so thick with shoots and so entangled with the mess that surrounded them. It was daunting to begin, but we did begin, spraying vinegar on the weeds first, so we could yank them more easily, then, armed with clippers, saws, shovels, but mostly just our gloved hands, yanking and hacking away.

I say we, but at first it was just me. HR was planting wildflowers around the rose bushes. Jessica, with her eleventh-month-old baby on her back and her five-year-old by her feet, was sawing the dead branches we hoped to turn to mulch. Sam was working the irrigation system. Petra was planting more spinach and carrots. I was sitting alone, cross legged in the shade of the tree, smelling mint and sage, pulling from the roots, then, when I got tired of sitting, standing to pull, then sitting again. There were so many weeds I didn't have to move much to get them, just shift a bit my angle and I'd meet a whole new crew.

But gradually I was moving in toward the trunk of the tree, into its dark cool center, which at first, I could not see. And then, there was an object. I startled. I was, of course, afraid, as if a suitcase out of place were a body out of place, and not just the sign of one. A suitcase—a pretty nice one, zipped up—a shoulder bag, also zipped, and a plastic bag holding a pair of sneakers. These items were neatly arranged, not tossed. They belonged to someone.

No body, though perhaps a body's markings, the weeds near the bags had been flattened. It seemed someone had been sleeping there in that quiet cave of leaves.

In May 2012 Denver's city council approved an Urban Camping Ban, an ordinance sponsored by Councilman Albus Brooks. Other cities have them. In fact, 34 percent of American cities ban camping in public, 18 percent ban sleeping in public.[2] Making it illegal to sleep outdoors means, to state the obvious, that those who are unhoused have to sleep in a shelter (that there are not enough beds does not even need to be said), risk arrest (and the subsequent criminal record as well as fines), or find a place to hide. Some cities don't have such bans and instead designate areas for the homeless to sleep, providing services in these locations, but Denver has gone the other way.

The building was for Counterpath, the nonprofit art and performance space my husband, Tim Roberts, and I run in which we'd recently hosted "Neighborhood History Day, "A Blind Date with Democracy," "The Open Opening" (to which anyone could to bring art to display, art of any kind), a feminism and philosophy conference dance party, the launch for eleven-year-old Patrick's online journal of jokes, magic spells, acrostics, and palindromes, and many other such events for poets, performers, activists, and artists. The garden was for anyone who wanted to work in it and eat from it. A portion of all food grown would be donated to soup kitchens in the area. The idea for the apples was that once we'd cleared the area around the trees we'd prune the trees back to health. I didn't know if it would work, but I hoped that then the trees would produce fruit in abundance again. And maybe the kids who lived on the block, Cornelius, Cordelia, Cortrelle, and Asian, or just anyone walking by, could eat that fruit next September and October, and I could make applesauce and pies.

But when I saw the bags I didn't know whether what I was currently doing made any sense. Gently, I pushed the bags further in—and what, exactly, did this accomplish?

Was there some lesson waiting to be learned from the suitcase under the tree, for example, or from the other thing on my mind—that I was clearing these weeds and making this garden in the immediate wake of a massacre—forty-nine people who went only to dance and to be with one another, mostly young, gay, trans, Latinx, all already by this country at this time made vulnerable for nothing but being? I was clearing these weeds and making this garden while every seventeen minutes somewhere in the country another person was shot. Though humble, and maybe stupidly so, I hoped that the clearing was a peaceful act, an act *for* peace, and not just a private one, one that would extend, more than many things I did, beyond me.

It seemed, even, there could be a parable, or more modestly a metaphor, in such clearing. And then there was, but it wasn't the metaphor I had imagined.

Days later the bags were still there, untouched, and still I did not remove them, even as I removed sage, brome, shepherd's purse, mint and cut the dead branches from the tree, cautiously, slowly now, with less certainty, less pride, trying not to cut any healthy branches, any with apples, failing in this regard.

I once had a friend named Itty Neuhaus, an artist who specialized in placing objects where they should not be. Her breakthrough work, "Padded Landing," suspended an entire car frame in a net from the underside of a bridge in New York City, traffic flowing overtop. This unlikely act, placing the car under instead of on the bridge, set her career in a particular direction. When I met her she was soaking the oddly named "husbands"—those pillows with the little arms that people used to lean on in bed. Itty placed three husbands in a kind of circle, like a witches' coven, and then, methodically, got them wet—sprinklers set up in the gallery to rain.

Itty was interested in the body, too, particularly the female body, because of how it swells and shrinks, in puberty, in pregnancy, but also just in the less predictable ways of weight gain or loss. The swollen soaked pillow, the suspended car, the distended body, and bread dough—one of her central materials in those years—all of these things in their ungainliness, their monstrosity, their escape, you could say, from form into new form, or formlessness, were her muse. Mostly, she was interested in instability or dissonance, how a house made of bread dough would rise and then rot, how a soaked pillow would expand and then collapse, and how placing an object where it did not belong made the space itself unstable, even untenable, no longer itself. All this came to mind as I considered the suitcase under the tree, unwilling to move it or look inside.

"The body presents the paradox of contained and container at once. Thus our attention is continually focused upon the boundaries or limits of the body," writes Susan Stewart in her essay "The Imaginary Body." And then later, "We want to know what is the body and what is not."[3]

But what if the body was never this thing—never a form that could be provoked or perverted into a monstrosity—entered and expanded, soaked or cut, and thereby unmade or made other? What if the form of the body or the form of the city is already not and will never be what we thought it was, what we are told it should be: a clarity, a perfection, a completion? What if there really is no shape of a tree to prune for, no garden to reinvent, and therefore no weed or brush to clear, no health or wholeness to return to?

In her seminal essay analyzing the particular cruxes of patriarchy and white supremacy in America, "Mama's Baby Papa's Maybe: An American Grammar Book," Hortense Spillers considers the difference between body and flesh. "But I would make a distinction in this case between 'body' and 'flesh' and impose that distinction as the central one between captive and liberated subject-positions," she begins, and then goes on to note William Goodell's 1853 study of the American Slave Code in which he details the precise acts of terror that will turn body to flesh:

> The smack of the whip is all day long in the ears of those who are on the plantation, or in the vicinity; and it is used with such dexterity and severity as not only to lacerate the skin, but to tear out small portions of the flesh at almost every stake.[4]

Reading this, or reading so many things available if we should seek them out, is to be reminded, if we need to be, that the fantasy of a whole and unruptured *social body* is a fantasy that rests, in the history of our country, against the forced flesh of the slave, just as the fantasy of the well-functioning affluent city, the dream city we are trying to make, is built on a foundation of criminality, on land that was only ever stolen.[5]

To discover the suitcase under the tree, to read the massacre's list of names, to remember that it is precisely when the border between inner and outer is broken that the body becomes flesh, is to know once more that the collective that is our dream-nation is *already* broken, already torn by its own brutality, both historic and present. To clear land Counterpath has purchased is, in some sense, in the context of our city, to add to such brutality, even as growing food for the families of our friends and neighbors, for the students, or for others who we do not know is some attempt to heal what we, even before such purchases were made, have already done or already are.[6]

My copy of William Carlos Williams's great book *Paterson* shows the signs of my needs. The pages are marked, post-its adorn it, dog-eared corners rip at their seams, fallen out pages have been stuck back in upside down or in the wrong place. I have written so much in its margins that it's almost a kind of journal.

What might be in that book that answers such needs, or, at least, describes them? The book, already a monstrosity, becomes more so each year that I pull it apart to teach it, to learn it, again. A book like that, read so many times, starts to draw apart from its author. It's not that it becomes mine, but that it becomes an appendage of myself, a growth of me from outside of me.

Paterson opens on monsters, a giant (the character "Paterson" himself) lying along the falls. And beyond him, "oozy fields / abandoned to grey beds of dead grass, / black sumac, withered weed-stalks, / mud and thickets cluttered with dead leaves—"[7]: a place a lot like the place I'm in, crammed with growth not wanted, or not called for, uncalled for excess that threatens to burst the word "field" or the word "garden" and destroy it.

A few pages later, we find "a monster in human form,"

he is twenty-seven years of age, his face from the upper part of his forehead to the end of his chin, measures *twenty-seven inches,* and around the upper part of his head is twenty-one inches: his eyes and nose are remarkably large and prominent, chin long and pointed. His features are coarse, irregular and disgusting, his voice rough and sonorous. His body is twenty-seven inches in length, his limbs are small and much deformed, and he has use of one hand only.[8]

This composite man who lies in a cradle but cracks jokes with clerics presents a problem of truth. Though this description is lifted directly from Neil Baldwin and Henry Howe's *Historical Collections of the State of New Jersey (1844)*, the coincidence of the number 27 makes of the man's "monstrosity" a myth and a metaphor. And indeed Williams provides us with what could be called his "tenor" in the very next prose paragraph, which details the town of Paterson's population just seventy years after Alexander Hamilton saw fit to fund its development into America's first planned industrial city:

> There were in 1870, native born 20,711, which would of course include children of foreign parents; foreign 12,868 of whom 237 were French, 1,429 German, 3,343 English—(Mr. Lambert who later built the Castle among them), 5,124 Irish, 879 Scotch, 1,360 Hollanders and 170 Swiss.[9]

That such rapid and diverse growth is seen by Williams as a kind of perversity is underscored by the third prose passage in the group. Here he borrows a news item from 1817 that describes the catching of an enormous 126-pound sturgeon under the heading "The Monster Taken."

But what is Williams's attitude toward these "monsters"? How are we to understand his feelings about his rapidly grown mash-up of a city (and book)? Such instability is, we learn, his source, his muse. The monstrous, the obscene—of poverty, but not only poverty, also grieving, age, sexuality, even childhood—provides him with the "things" or "facts" he needs to write from.

> A delirium of solutions, forthwith, forces
> him into back streets, to begin again:
> up hollow stairs among acrid smells
> to obscene rendezvous. And there he finds
> a festering sweetness of red lollipops-
> and yelping dog:
> Come YEAH, Chichi! Or a great belly
> that no longer laughs but mourns
> with its expressionless black navel love's
> deceit . . .

They are the divisions and imbalances
of his whole concept, made weak by pity,
flouting desire, they are—No ideas but
in the facts . . .[10]

A man cares for a younger man in the café where I write. The
man being cared for doesn't speak, rocks back and forth, makes
unexpected and loud noises, stands suddenly and bursts for the
door. In another age he might have been considered dangerous,
he might have been kept away, he might not have been cared
for at all. Today, the man caring for him catches his elbow, gen-
tly restraining. The younger man, groaning, pushes the other's
hand off, so that the caring man takes his waist instead. Again
pushed off. Standing in the way of the door, he speaks urgently
but quietly: "I'm down with going wherever you want to go, but
you just have to tell me, you can't just jump up!" After a longer
struggle involving various attempts to bolt, the first man coaxes
the other back to the couch where they settle, finally, into read-
ing. The agitated man is lying down now, his head resting in the
lap of his caretaker. The reading man's hand lies on the other's
forehead exactly as if checking for a fever. He reads out loud,
pausing to drink from his water bottle (using only his reading
hand, not moving the other from the forehead), until finally the
other man is asleep. The first man continues to read, but now
silently, with the younger man's head in his lap.

A week later Counterpath sets up our performance tent at
City Park Jazz, the free summer concerts we'd been invited to
collaborate with. For ten consecutive weekends we publish a
chapbook that corresponds with a performance or installation
in the tent. This time two dancers, Lauren Beale and Brooke
McNamara, dressed in golden bathing suits, perform; the tent's
been set up to look like a fifties living room. Meanwhile, Hazel
Miller sings on stage, and I wander down through the picnicking
people so that I can also dance with the collective of kids, cou-
ples, and folks on their own, barefoot or in cocktail dresses, in
their flamboyant freestyle or dance-class swing. There I see the
young man from the café, dancing with a woman who appears
to be his mother. She moves her body in a kind of semicircle of

protection, dancing with him, but also around him, so that, I guess, he can't easily bolt. But he doesn't seem to want to, they are having so much fun. Her necklace of beads swings free of her chest; his curls bob. Their private agreement extends into the crowd; everyone gives them a little extra room, as if dancing were a brief and contingent healing, a slipping stroke, and care itself only and ever a momentary and minor gesture.

Williams's interest in dissonant, out-of-place, or monstrous events and entities runs throughout the five books of *Paterson*. One could say it is the work's central theme. A lake bed writhing with eels, a man's body caught between logs and dangling above the falls, a dead horse in the sewer, the "deformed and mutilated verses" of the Greek poet Hipponax, the monstrous acts of the natural world—fires, floods, and earthquakes—and of the human—murders and rapes.

Significantly, one of Williams's later objects of fascination is the irradiated and pregnant body of Marie Curie, her "fetid womb"—a metaphor for the world itself—which occupies the better part of the second section of Book IV, dated 1951. But to say "metaphor" is too simple here. In the fourth book of Paterson "constellation" is probably the better term, as womb/world/ bomb/atom/and book link together, versions of one another or parts of a whole. One could say that in this section, Williams's interest in monstrosity becomes monstrous in itself, as physics and chemistry in their most heinous application become symbolic of human and creative transformation. Or, as Williams put it, rather horrifically in 1948, "one great thing about 'the bomb' is the awakened sense it gives us that catastrophic . . . alterations are also possible in the human *mind*, in art, in the arts. . . . We are too cowed by our fears to realize it fully. But it is *possible*. That is what we mean. This isn't optimism, it is chemistry: Or better, physics."[11] As Marianne Borruch acerbically noted in 1985, "It's hard to think straight—that is kindly—about such remarks."[12] And yet, with Borruch and others, we recognize that Williams was not blithe in his engagement with science, whether medical or atomic. The engagement was deep, and the connections he tried to draw between twentieth-century eruptions in science and those he instigated in poetry were in no way trivial. Further, his relationship to the bomb as "image" shifts significantly over the years. In *Paterson* we find an early, hesitant, and in many ways uninformed application. But for this reason in particular, I turn to it, trying to find there an indication of what a poetics of dissonance, of fission, of monstrosity might deliver. Perhaps even more to discover "How the twentieth-century mind becomes alert to its own recklessness" (Boruch)[13] in order to become more alert to my own.

The section opens on a rare scene of paternal attention. Williams remembers taking his teenaged son to a lecture on atomic fission. And yet, this scene begins quickly to break apart into a confused or "fetid" swarm of references—parenthood, poetry, Curie and the 1943 film *Madame Curie,* Billy Sunday's evangelism, and finally a letter from Williams's other (true?) son, Allen Ginsberg. At one point a "poem" emerges, recognizable as such by way of indentation and Williams's use of his "triadic-line":

A dissonance
in the valence of Uranium
led to the discovery

Dissonance
(if you are interested)
leads to discovery

—to dissect away
the block and leave
a separate metal:

hydrogen
the flame, helium the
pregnant ash[14]

This description of the transmutation of the unstable element uranium was published, of course, in the wake of Nagasaki and Hiroshima. And yet, the "dissonance" of uranium is evoked here, as throughout, more for its potential to bring forth the new—for the "pregnancy" of its ash—than for the cataclysmic damage that its "little boy" had, only a few years prior, wreaked upon an entire nation.

Images of perverse or violent (re)production occur over this handful of pages with an alarming range. Here is just a partial list: a nurse with abdominal "disturbances"; Curie's own laboring mind, her "ponderous belly, full / of thought"; the city itself, "that complex atom / always breaking down"; the sun parting the "labia" of the "shabby" clouds (echoing the rapes of previous pages); and finally, the developing debt required to fund the Cold War, which Williams equates with uranium, presumably for how debt is both generative and destructive. None of this resolves. To resolve would be, in fact, to belie the aesthetics of fissure, which only wants to mushroom outward and upward in never-ending expansion, just as the "spreading" "splendor" of America's cities grows and grows, fueled by the "radiant gist" that is national or personal debt.[15] Which is to say, in this section of *Paterson* we are given to understand the core of violence that both sustains and damns the fecundity we enjoy.

Property values in Denver have been rising this decade at faster rates than in any other non-coastal city in the country, marginally outpaced only by Seattle, Portland, and San Francisco. In 2015, the average home price in Denver is $500,000, with one-bedroom apartments within a ten-mile radius of the city averaging $1,600 a month in rent. Meanwhile, a full-time minimum-wage worker earns just $1,300 a month (the problem is growing increasingly worse).[16] On Colfax Avenue, one block north of the garden, runs a two-mile stretch of one- and two-story motels: Sand and Sage, Airway Motel, The Branding Iron, The Driftwood. These motels with their evocative names are the topic of much conversation at neighborhood meetings. On the one hand, prostitution and drug-related activities, on the same hand, homeless families.[17] There are currently 23,300 documented homeless students in Colorado's public schools, a number that has tripled during the same decade Denver has "enjoyed" its real-estate boom.

Here's to the baby,
may it thrive!
Here's to the labia
that rive

to give it place
in a stubborn world.
And here's to the peak
from which the seed was hurled![18]

This brief and aggressive celebration of sexual reproduction
from Book IV is nestled between two tributes, the first to the
Passaic River: "My serpent, great river! genius of the fields," and
the second, an almost verbatim steal from an early twentieth-
century text titled *A Little Story of Old Paterson as Told by an Old
Man*, which describes the town of Paterson as it might have
looked circa 1700. The striking aspects of these otherwise pasto-
ral idylls are the vicious histories they almost casually allude to.
For the tribute to the river opens with a reported conversation
with a "Jap": "Yellow, for genius, the Jap said. Yellow / is your
color."[19] We are reminded, if elusively and with unclear inten-
tions, of the period's anti-Japanese sentiment. We are reminded
too of the true horrors of the bomb that in previous pages has
only been discussed in scientific or metaphoric terms. This is, in
fact, Williams's only mention or allusion to Japan, and though
it is unclear what work he thought it was doing, the moment
presents an undeniable and bitter cry. The passages taken from
A Little Story nostalgically mention "branching trees and ample
gardens," but also make reference to "The wigwam and the
tomahawk, the Totowa tribe" as well as to the "colored slaves"
of eighteenth-century Paterson.[20] Again, intentionality is vague,
but effect is clear. There is no growth, no Paterson at all (as
there is no Denver), without the stolen lands and stolen bodies
beneath, behind, and within its history.

What am I to do, then, with this book and its strained and "vul-
gar" attempts to bring together, between its pages, the brutally
murdered, the beaten, the silenced, the disregarded, the forgot-
ten and violent histories of a town all while it attempts to make
of such monstrosities an adequate and productive metaphor for
writing?

Paterson dwells in monstrosity in order to find in difference a
source of energy, even health. But, despite how uranium's "dis-
sonance" seems so conveniently to fall within the range of dis-

sonances Williams celebrates, the bomb can never *be* an image, can never really *be* a metaphor. And perhaps no act of violence, no matter how local, how precise, how unintentional, can be harnessed for its metaphoric uses without doing further damage to the flesh that suffers.

Counterpath took root in a rented storefront, a building purchased in 2014 by developers who immediately quintupled the rent. We were lucky enough to buy outright the 1954 gas station, drawing on tax-deductible donations from Tim's business in university press publishing and the recent sale of a building that had housed my father's business (the architecture firm of Stephen Carr and Kevin Lynch, themselves seminal theorists of participatory urban design) for over thirty years. The diseased tree hiding the baggage that I will not open, that belongs to someone who does not return for it, grows along the border between public and private land, though in fact, the property, being owned not by us but by the nonprofit that is Counterpath, hovers between these two poles.[21] The tree's seeming illness, its monstrosity, how it is barely recognizable as a tree, is, it now seems, a kind of health for how it has sheltered someone's survival. And yet even this health hides a greater illness, for it's a city's lack of structural care that makes such fragile temporary shelter a solution.

In my effort to heal the tree, cutting layers of blight away branch by branch, I perform a service and a disservice. In pruning it I find myself unwittingly enacting the very "pruning" that my city has chosen as law. "To be situated in a position of greater social power produces the social privilege of not seeing how the interests and concerns associated with one's . . . social location have deeply informed the physical and social world to the disadvantage of those occupying different social locations," I read,[22] and do not know what to do. It had seemed that if I could heal the tree, then I could heal something else as well. It had seemed that the apple tree in its eternal metaphors might, once producing fruit, represent the hope for a healed body, a healed city, a healed country. And in that dream, children emerge from the houses—my children, the children of my students and friends, the children from across the street, and those in the motels on

Colfax—they all come to eat. But the tree was never really a metaphor, or its metaphor was, by me, misread. Porous, soaked, rotting, blighted, sending out shoots, trying to live, the knowledge it offered was not waiting to be uncovered like some pure and virginal body, but was there all along within its depths, in its imperfections, in its flesh.

Notes

1. Wendy Brown et al., "Learning to Love Again: An Interview with Wendy Brown," *Contretemps* 6 (January 2006): 26, accessed May 26, 2017, http://sydney.edu.au/contretemps/6January2006/brown.pdf.

2. Tony Robinson and Alison Sickels, *No Right to Rest: Criminalizing Homelessness in Colorado,* Denver Homeless Outloud, 20, accessed May 26, 2017, https://denverhomelessoutloud.files.wordpress.com/2016/03/no-right-2-rest.pdf.

3. Susan Stewart, "The Imaginary Body," in *On Longing: Narratives of the Miniature, the Gigantic, the Souvenir, the Collection* (Durham, NC: Duke University Press, 1992), 104, 105.

4. Hortense Spillers, "Mama's Baby, Papa's Maybe: An American Grammar Book," in *Black, White and in Color: Essays on American Literature and Culture* (Chicago: University of Chicago Press, 2003), 207.

5. Who is the "we" that needs reminding? Anne-Lise Francois speaks of the "open secret" as that readily available information that only those with power can choose not to see. What I'm calling Spiller's "reminder" of the material history of flesh making will only be a reminder to those of us who can, for reasons of wealth or whiteness or both, afford to forget. Anne-Lise Francois, *Open Secrets: The Literature of Uncounted Experience* (Palo Alto, CA: Stanford University Press, 2007).

6. My own great-grandfather, Omer Madison Kem, was a homesteader, moving from Indiana, where he'd been a destitute farmer, to the "free land" in Nebraska, free for whites because taken from the Otoe Indians. This land he also failed to farm. Instead he turned to the anticapitalist Populist party, running for and winning a seat in the House of Representatives, which he held from 1891 to 1897. The success of his political career allowed him to purchase land near Montrose, Colorado, the former home of the Ute Indians. On this land he, like his great-granddaughter, attempted to raise apples.

7. Williams, *Paterson*, 7.

8. Ibid., 10.

9. Ibid, 10.

10. Ibid., 27.

11. Williams, "The Poem as a Field of Action," Poetry Foundation, accessed May 25, 2017, https://www.poetryfoundation.org/resources/learning/essays/detail/69393.

12. Marianne Boruch, "Williams and the Bomb," in *In the Blue Pharmacy: Essays on Poetry and Other Transformations* (San Antonio, TX: Trinity University Press, 2005), 38.

13. Ibid., 41.

14. Williams, *Paterson*, 175.

15. Ibid., 176–85.

16. Statistics from Denver Homeless Outloud and Chad Kautzer eds., *The Struggle for Space: Homelessness and the Politics of Dys-appearance in American Cities,* Denver Homeless Outloud, 27, accessed May 25, 2017, https://denverhomelessoutloud.files.wordpress.com/2016/05/bien nialdholbooklet.pdf.

17. These motels are also the topic of the excellent short documentary film Colfax Motels, by Corky Scholl, accessed May 25, 2017, https://www.youtube.com/watch?v=rqBaMuBdoKU.

18. Williams, *Paterson*, 192.

19. Ibid.

20. Ibid., 193–94.

21. Because the property belongs to Counterpath, we as individuals can never profit from its sale. Any profit would have to be folded back into the organization. This legal detail does not, however, make any difference at all to the person who had been sleeping under the tree.

22. Kautzer, "Homelessness, Dys-Appearance and Resistance," in *The Struggle for Space,* 12.

Interview with Rob Mclennan for
Touch the Donkey supplement #7
Seven Questions for Julie Carr,
June 2014

ROB MCLENNAN: Tell me about the work-in-progress *Real Life: An Installation*. How did it originate?

JULIE CARR: Like a lot of poets, I found myself in a situation where I had a number of manuscripts sort of lined up, ready to send out or even slotted for publication, and it seemed to be happening too fast, like whirring by without enough time to absorb and process. It was the summer of 2011, and my partner Tim said to me, you need something to write that will take you at least five years. In response I created a process for myself—I would write every day from Labor Day to Labor Day to Labor Day, beginning in 2011. I did not allow myself to read back what I'd written, except at three-month intervals, and then I could do only very slight cleaning for spelling and stuff. That way I was always writing into an unknown, forgetting what I'd done the day before, keeping it strange and off-balance. Of course themes and forms emerged, but they'd shift pretty regularly, and I had to allow that, since I was not editing at all. At the end of the two years, I had twelve sections and a total of almost 600 pages. Now I am editing, forming, shaping, and cutting most of it. The editing process will take at least as long as the original writing, probably longer.

The title came from my daughter, who was four when I started. She'd often refer to things and events as "real life," in order to distinguish them from what was happening in her imagination, in her dreams, or in stories and movies. For kids at that age it's important to clarify, since so much is going on all the time that is not "real life" (and they are often unsure what is and what isn't real). I started to notice that when adults use the phrase "real life" they usually mean work, or the mundane, the everyday, as opposed to art, sex, love, illness, dreams, play. Pretty much anything that is any fun or has any intensity attached to it qualifies as not real life! I thought I'd trouble the term, while also thinking a lot about labor, work, and economics throughout the writing.

I began thinking about installation art because I always am, but also because of a talk Fredric Jameson gave in which he claimed that the artists of the future will all be installation artists, or something like that. I can say more about that if you like.

RM: Certainly!

JC: What I remember from Jameson's talk (and I think this is a talk he'd been giving a lot that year around the country) was the idea that 1) we are in a time of rampant presentism with no clear or even muddy vision for the future and no memory of the past, and 2) that all artists are now curators or installation artists, gathering materials and arranging them, rather than making them. I don't agree with either of these ideas, though certainly I can see where they come from. Instead I see a lot of people struggling to imagine new futures and working toward them (in art and activism), and I see a lot of really relevant art that is in no way "just" a gathering together or curation. Nonetheless, the idea struck me enough to make me want to explore directly what it might mean to think of my writing as installation art. Often, long before hearing this talk (and this is probably because of my theater/dance background), I've imagined or dreamed my poems happening in spaces. I hear the voice recorded, see some kind of event or dance or architectural structure that illuminates, supports, or otherwise *is* the poem.

When I was little I used to love, almost more than anything 1) amusement parks and 2) the plaster Easter eggs where you can peer into one end and see a little scene of bunnies and kids in spring clothing, or whatever. Both of these are installations, big and small, created worlds. I think I want my writing to act like that.

And so, *Real Life* has many imagined installations running through it, some that could be constructed, and others that could not.

RM: Your five poetry collections, including *RAG* (Omnidawn, 2014) are each constructed as large, expansive book-length projects as well. How does this current project relate to what you've produced before? How is it different?

JC: You're right about that! One day perhaps I'll write a book of discrete poems—what Spicer called one night stands. But for now, this is how my mind works. Right now I'd say that *Real Life* is different because of the process of creating it. I want to hold off on understanding for as long as possible, to keep it unstable and unknown. So far that has been the case—it is too long and too wide for me to be able to see the whole of it. Eventually I assume that won't be true, but for now it seems important to be patient, to let it unfold to me very slowly. There are certain topics that I find urgent and modes of expression that I've explored in relation to those topics. Here I want to push myself to find a way to not settle too quickly. I should say that there are two other books coming out before this one, and I've been working hard on these as well, so *Real Life* has also been a kind of background project at times, a form of meditation, a practice, ongoing and continuously strange. I've also been writing these other things with very different modes of attack.

RM: I like that you're allowing your uncertainty to develop, and not letting the conscious mind interfere with what the unconscious mind is creating. I'm curious about your development into utilizing the book as your unit of composition (as opposed to the poem). How did this evolve? You mention Jack Spicer, but who (else) are your models?

JC: I'd say my first influence in working this way was Lyn Hejinian. I read her first when I was about 27, and she blew my mind. Before reading *My Life* I had a very different idea of what a book was and what it could do. I was into minimalism, abstraction, the odd meditations of René Char, Tomaž Šalamun, Denise Levertov, Emily Dickinson. *My Life* broke something open for me, even though I still love all those authors. Also, early on I read Michael Palmer quite a lot, and his sequences were a big influence as well. Cole Swensen's work was a huge influence on my first and second books—especially her *Noon,* which I read constantly for at least a year.

After that, Zukofsky's *"A"* and Vallejo's *Trilce*—both of which I read with others over long periods of time. These reading experiences were so rich, unprecedented in their slowness and depth. I'm so grateful to the people in that reading group for the time we spent with those authors. Williams' *Paterson* is one of my favorite works to teach and reread. I love it for its struggles and all that is unresolved there. And Olson's *Maximus* has also been wonderful to spend time with, to teach, to attempt to get inside. More contemporary writers that have influenced me in this way include Eleni Sikelianos—her *California Poem* especially (in terms of form—I love all her work), and Anne Carson for how she blends genres and forms throughout books. And of course, C. D. Wright and Nathaniel Mackey.

RM: A number of the works you mention engage with narrative and personal information in rather interesting ways. How conscious are you about including your personal and domestic life in the conversation of your writing? Is this something you think might change as your daughter ages, and begins to gain awareness of how she is being depicted? What are your boundaries?

JC: Well, first, there are three kids, and the oldest is 16. Just for the record.

I feel like there's a question inside your question. Maybe something like—is it ethical (or polite) to depict one's kids in one's work? So, yes, I think it is fine, inevitable, and important. Because I'm interested in the human, in all of life, which must include relations, especially those most intimate (but not only), it would be entirely false of me to somehow exclude children from writing.

I'm not at all interested in writing that places boundaries around what can and can't be written about. That said, I would not reveal someone else's secrets, or willfully embarrass a child or anyone else. When I've had questions about my material—about whether it embarrasses a person or reveals something they don't want revealed, I simply show it to that person and ask them directly. So my boundary is exactly that—I let the person decide and only one time has a person said "No. Please don't include that." Sometimes I haven't anticipated any reaction, and have been wrong about that. I've made mistakes, but not in writing about the kids specifically.

All three kids are aware that "they" appear in poems, and sometimes, in fact, their own poems have appeared in my books—credited of course. I think they understand what others also understand: that all of "real life" is filtered when written.

It is and isn't truth. It is and isn't them. They write about me too (and definitely make things up)! And even when they say things that are not true to me, I understand that what they write is true to the writing. I'm pretty sure everyone around here has a healthy understanding of writing as complex in its relation to truth.

As for the first part of the question—there are so many issues that this brings up, I hardly know where to begin. First, I'll say that the question is loaded for me with concerns around gender. Women have historically been shamed out of writing the "personal," or shamed for writing about "domestic" issues (read Barrett Browning's *Aurora Leigh* for a great satirical attack on the way women's writing has been mocked for being too involved in intimate matters). I resist that shaming and I resist any division between the personal and the political or the private and the public, because all of these divisions are gendered, and have been for hundreds of years. My personal and domestic life is my civic life, is my political life, is my public life. There is no way that my house is not political: it speaks about class, it speaks about education, it speaks about race. There's no way my work as a teacher or a publisher is not intimate. That work speaks about love, desire, friendship, and emotion.

One of the thrusts of *Real Life: An Installation* is to put pressure on the very question you are asking—but I've been putting pressure on that question ever since my first book, and I suppose I'll always be doing that.

RM: I like hearing that your children are writing, and that you are including—credited of course—some of their poems in your books. What do you think you've learned about writing, whether generally or your own, from your children? What have you discovered through seeing your own work through their perspectives?

JC: I learn from them that it's great when you can write each letter in a different color.

And here's an anecdote: when my middle daughter was about six she drew a self-portrait around which she wrote the words "There is no escaping me." My youngest's first written sentence was "I like myself" (I lak m sef). This has something to do with their personalities. But also, both of these statements are useful for writing. Whatever and whoever we are, that's always going to be in the writing no matter how hard we might try to depersonalize it. There is no escaping the self, so you might as well face it. On the other hand, as I was saying to some friends yesterday, writing is this strange process of constantly coaxing ourselves to fall back in love with ourselves (or at least to like ourselves), because if we are too disgusted we just can't do it. So there's this facing and this forgiving that have to happen all the time.

RM: After five published poetry collections (as well as this current work-in-progress), how do you feel your work has developed? What, if anything, do you feel you are working toward?

JC: This is a hard question to approach. One doesn't like to sum up one's work or to claim goals that will inevitably shift anyway. Also, I resist narratives of progress in relation to making art. But I do know that for a while I've been setting a goal, in one way or another, of more range, freedom, or wildness. At the same time, I'm also interested in how each book creates its own boundaries, whether in terms of form or content. A book ends up describing itself and I'm trying to be aware of what each given project wants to do or be.

To be a bit more specific, I'm working toward a couple of prose books right now (in addition to *Real Life*, and another book of very short poems, *Think Tank*, coming out soon from Solid Objects). I'm trying to teach myself to write essays I'd want to read. And, to that end, I'm studying various writers who push the essay form. One of these books is on the topic of confession (literary confession, more or less). The other is a collection of essays about poetry and affect, which will take me a long time to finish.

I guess if I could say anything about what I'm reaching for I'd say maximal range, maximal intensity, and more patience. And one day I'd like to write a novel, maybe when I am very old.

Interview with Sofi Thanhauser for
Entropy magazine, June 7, 2016

SOFI THANHAUSER: One of the things you seem to be doing in
[the chapbook of essays titled] *The Silence That Fills the Future*[1] is
claiming the simultaneous co-existence of a self constructed by
and through narrative and a type of *presence* that exists outside
of (and in some ways calls the lie on) that narrative self. The
binary I'm offering is clumsy, and I don't mean to offer clumsily
what you've already performed deftly. What I'm asking is, do
you see the assemblage itself: the gathering together and the
ordering of the four works that comprise *The Silence That Fills
the Future,* as a kind demonstration or performance of the way
in which we live both inside and outside the narrative of self?
Maybe even as a kind of rapprochement between those two
locations? I experienced it that way. Reading this chapbook
made me more comfortable with my own experience of
navigating those two terrains. I hope this can be read as a
question and not merely a compliment. If it can't, I'll try again
with another one.

JULIE CARR: I like this question a lot. Let me see what I can do with
it.

I'm going to answer this more generally, since for me the
collection of those pieces feels provisional, like a resting point
before the release of a few books in the future (hence the
title). But in general what I would say is that for me writing
itself is always an experience, or as you say "performance," of
that navigation—the navigation between a narrativised self and
a self that refuses to be narrated. The self that refuses might
be the self of sensation, presence, the body when experienced
as itself, rather than as a walking emblem of the story of the
self. But I want to resist hierarchies here. It's not that one is
more authentic than the other; we have to narrate ourselves
to ourselves, we have to become, in that way literary, otherwise

how would we function? How would we make meaning of the world, and how would we judge it and find ways to change it?

In some ways writing is particularly useful to us. It helps us "make sense," and therefore it helps us make claims. But at the same time, in its improvisatory mode, writing is how we register the moment-to-moment awareness, the animal in us that just takes in and responds immediately. I don't know if this is true, since I've been writing as long as I knew how, but I think it might be true that it's harder to be aware of the dynamic between these two poles without writing or in some other way recording these processes as they occur.

Poetry seems especially suited for these recordings because it offers escapes from narrative even as it enjoys narrative or argument when it wants to.

Today when I think about a narrativised self, I think of the self in relation to structures: the family, the institution, the state. There exists a desire to escape all that, if even only (and importantly) in one's mind. Perhaps the recording of narrative-resistant experience is, in part, the record of institutional resistance.

ST: I'm interested in the ethical component of the "narrativised self" that you raise. In "By Beauty and By Fear: On Narrative Time" you write, "a poem, then, is an anti-narrative, which might be a good reason to fear it, or, if narratives lead only to horror or loss, might be a good reason to court it." When I first read these lines the choice seemed totally clear to me (court it, court it!). But this ethical component you raise is chastening. If the self that hurts and experiences loss is the same one that has responsibilities and the capacity for action, it isn't viable to jump ship on the self, however tempting that may be. I'd like to put this in conversation with some other lines from "By Beauty and By Fear: On Narrative Time":

"Let me in," say the women, picking at their food.
For even more frightening than a narrative that features
    depravity is having no narrative at all.

When I read these lines I felt a certain shudder of recognition. I had never before thought to connect the way in which I feel I have no narrative with the fact of being female. It seems like in "By Beauty and By Fear: On Narrative Time" you are raising the paradox that this navigation (between self outside of and inside of narrative) is deeply personal but is also acted out in relation to others, to society, to history, to cultural inheritance. And that there is bravery required! Can you speak to this?

JC: I think the sense that the narrativized self is both a burden and a choice comes more readily to those whose narratives have been written for them. Only 7–13% of all (Hollywood) film directors are female, about the same percentage for writers and only 5% of cinematographers. In television it's a little better, but still less than a quarter of creative work in TV is done by women. These percentages only tell a tiny fraction of the story, because so often the narratives we encounter about women are damaging, whether they be found in texts of various kinds, or just in the standard flow of images we deal with which describe us or attempt to make us. When you have daughters you see what this is really about. The girls have to fight against so many images (and images are narratives) from day one. They have to contend with such pressures and it's hard; it's a burden that is constantly part of their lives. The same and much more can be said about the way in which our culture has narrated the lives of people of color, but from where I stand I can speak with more authority about (white) female experience.

Something about poetry allows relief from these narratives that both keep us out and make us specific. The freedoms of poetry are infinite. The range, the field, the ability to create, uncreate, recreate, undo and un-commit are, I think, absolutely crucial for anyone pushing against a culture's desire to limit and describe. I was just reading a great essay on the black and gay artist Glenn Ligon's work in which the author, Huey Copeland, argues that Ligon turns to language in his work as a way to find "refuge" (Copeland's word) from the violence of images that have been imposed upon the black body. I would suggest that the abstracted or in some way deranged language of poetry provides such refuge more readily than the familiar turns of narrative. And yet, I love fiction, and I want in. Why?

I think of Keats who wrote so beautifully about the freedom from "self" that poetry provides ("A Poet is the most unpoetical of any thing in existence; because he has no Identity—he is continually in for—and filling some other Body—The Sun, the Moon, the Sea and Men and Women. . . . It is a wretched thing to confess; but is a very fact that not one word I ever utter can be taken for granted as an opinion growing out of my identical nature—how can it, when I have no nature?"), but then worries

175

in other letters and poems about the ethical responsibilities of the poet. He worries that by being a poet he will only be a bane and not a balm upon the world, only an idle "dreamer." I think this worry is what draws poets to activism and to prose. It's not enough to escape. You also have to argue. Even when escape from normative prose is a kind of argument, is a kind of refusal that is in itself political, there is still a way that one finds direct engagement is necessary. Think of the work that [Claudia] Rankine's *Citizen* does. The moments that the reviewers quote, that everyone talks about, are moments of pure narrative. The book also has some much more poetic language that I find as compelling and powerful, but people rarely talk about that. It's not as clearly readable as "argument." Both, to me, are necessary. Rare to find both in one book!

And so poets write poems and then write pages and pages of prose (like this)!

ST: It's interesting what you say about the response to *Citizen.* I recently reread *A Room of One's Own* and *Three Guineas,* and was surprised to realize/remember that in addition to offering very sharp and prescient political/economic critiques, both are filled with moments of psychedelic poetry. But that isn't how they're canonized or taught! It's as though we can't handle poetry when it arrives within an essay or an argument, and choose to ignore it for the sake of categorization. In a way that's what my first question was trying to do with/to *your* work: unify and flatten it rather than accept it as an experience that transcends the fact or facts of its thesis. While I am on Woolf, I wanted to ask about some resonances I felt in this chapbook. The line:

Take off my face

from "A 14-line poem on progressive insurance" reminded me very much of Rhoda's "I have no face" in Woolf's *The Waves.* And the line:

Because I'm a child who outlives her mother

from "The War Reporter: On Confession" felt like the incredibly muted way in which the death of Mrs. Ramsay arrives in *To the Lighthouse.* Is there a real affinity here?

JC: So, yes, I read Woolf a lot when I was younger and her writing and ideas certainly influenced me, as I think they do everyone who reads her. But there is no direct response to those books in the writing—at least no conscious one!

Your question makes me want to re-read *The Waves*, though!

I don't think prose's relationship with poetry is an antagonistic one. Rather, I think what poetry does is push our thinking, and prose (or conversation) is how we try to articulate that in a more overt, and therefore public, way. In my own work that dynamic between rhetoric, or discursive language, and poetry is pretty active.

st: It certainly is! I'm fascinated with the mode by which these essays progress. I'm thinking especially of the "Beauty" section in "By Beauty and By Fear: On Narrative Time." It has a sort of straightforwardly dialectical movement at first, moving from Wordsworth's conception of beauty as the mind's effort to "make coherent sense out of what it fears," to the idea that beauty may be something that *cannot* tame fear and that is in fact in league with violence (which you illustrate with this wonderful motif of Aphrodite choosing Aries over Hephaestus!), to beauty as something that *might* be able to save (the "fragile, temporary, wild beauty of song") and might not. And then the essay gathers this unbelievable momentum:

"Wild nights-Wild Nights!"

and cascades towards this idea that "emotions, once set into action, continue indefinitely like entropic molecules." To me, it seems like a flawless construction and I can't find the seams. I am wondering if you have a method or mode, or even an operative metaphor that helps you write your way through an essay like this—to make these wild leaps and still produce something cohesive, balanced, elegant.

jc: Thank you! That essay took so long, and every time I read it I revised it. All I can say is that I began with the title, wanting to write about this line in Wordsworth and at the same time to think about fear and how for a while it was governing my life. I don't remember the stages or steps along the way, but I do know that I struggled mightily, and still do, with how much to control, how much to associate—with freedom and limit— in the essay form. In poems the same issues arise, but I think I've pretty much decided to trust a poem's intuitive leaps, even though when making a book I'm often worrying about how far afield I can go without losing a central core or focus. With essays the form requires so much more in the way of development, and that's something I want. I want to make an argument, to develop an idea. But then I also want that thing to happen where the reader follows and it feels right, but she isn't sure how she got from A-Z, because for me this has been an incredibly pleasurable part of reading. When it works it means I am giving myself over, trusting the writer, and in this way I am allowing myself to learn.

Some of the essays that inspire me for these reasons are Lisa Robertson's (in *Nilling* especially), and Kazim Ali's (he has a new book of essays out now titled *Resident Alien*), and the prose of Fred Moten. When I can predict the structure of an essay or feel that it's too neatly put together, I get bored, even irritated. There's a lot of those too.

ST: Part of the idea behind Essay Press' EP series is to allow authors space in which to present a preliminary or excerpted version of a longer work. In your introduction, you present each of the four sections of *The Silence That Fills the Future* as "future books, or dream events, or landscapes, or recording sessions, or fantasy vacations, or destroyed works, or small businesses, or emotion maps, or warm mirrors, or phantom cities, or provisional assertions, or architectural models, or cheap motels or late night bus rides." Can you say a little bit about what has happened in the life of each of these four sections, since the publication of *The Silence That Fills the Future*?

JC: "The War Reporter: On Confession" is the centerpiece to a new book that will be out with Ahsahta Press in 2017. The book is titled *Objects from a Borrowed Confession*. It's a series of prose pieces circling around the idea of confession. There's a novella, a number of essays, some poem/essays, an experiment in memoir, and a letter. "By Beauty and By Fear: On Narrative Time" is the second to last piece in that book.

"Spirit Ditties of No Tone: On Listening" is biding its time in an essay collection I've been trying to finish. Its working title is *Someone Shot my Book*. For a while it's been focused on feminism and emotion. I think I might have different ideas about emotion now and so will have to rethink the book. This one has been in the works for a long time, maybe five years. It's ok with me to have a book on a very slow burn. As I write more essays I see if they are part of it or not. Slowly, it comes together.

The fourteen-line poems are an aspect of another book I'm

writing now titled *Real Life: An Installation.* This project has been obsessing me since I embarked on it near the end of 2011. I hope to be done in about a year. At the moment it's an almost 500 page manuscript, 100 pages of which rest under my left elbow as I type. The fourteen-line poems form a kind of quick and clean break from some of the heavier material in the book, kind of like a sip of sake. When everything else in that book seems to be dying under its own weight, these still seem alive.

ST: I can certainly sympathize with the idea of material dying under its own weight. I think its pretty common for writers to use language to describe their own work that gives that work life and agency of its own. That's how it feels, maybe that's how it *is.* But if we were to take that personification or animation of the work very seriously for a moment, how would you conceive of, or cast yourself within the relationship with a work? For example, is it a relationship in which you must assert your dominance? Your submission? Something totally outside of that binary?

JC: Yeah, neither dominance nor submission. I think it's about not being afraid of it and trusting it. I guess I have this feeling that where the work fails, where it is too timid or boring or the tone is off, it's me not listening to and trusting it enough, that it's always there talking to me and I just have to be courageous in listening to it. Just now I wrote something called "My Mother's Ass." I could have censored it, not because I'm embarrassed to talk about my mother's ass, but because something about doing so seemed so obvious. But then I've learned not to judge things because they are obvious, so I allowed it. I think actually I was afraid of it for its anger (it's also about rape), and now that it's there, I'm glad I trusted it. I think it *is* weird that we divide the work from ourselves in this way, but I think it's what writers have always done. The work is not "us" but it comes from us and from around us, like some ideas of God. So, definitely not dominance, and yet I don't feel I am submitting because I don't experience it as a violence. But you know when you are listening to someone who is saying some scary shit, you kind of want them to shut up but you hold your tongue because you know there is truth there? That is what it's like.

ST: I'm thinking about what you said about being ok with having a book on "a very slow burn" and also what you write in the introduction to *The Silence That Fills the Future:* "For years I only worked on one or two projects at a time. I could not understand people who flipped back and forth between files on their computers like birds feeding various nests at once. But as the future looks shorter to me now than it did then, I begin, for better or worse, to cram more into the days or into the computer." Both of these raise questions about pace. I'm curious about how you think about pace, both in your work and in the broadest sense: how the pace of work proceeds within the pace of a whole career, a whole life.

JC: Good question. I don't know! This is one of the hardest things for me because actually I'm very impatient and compulsive, so slowness is hard. But I do know that rushing things generally does not produce the best results. Rushing is tied to ambition and to the desire to be liked, and both of these things will probably produce work that is somewhat shallow and false. So slowness is important for honesty. But I've also watched how different moments lend themselves to more or less productivity and I'm learning to accept that. You'd think that with three kids I would have accepted it long ago, but actually it's only been in recent years with my mother's death and my older kids becoming teenagers that I've begun to shift my relationship to time. I do feel this urgency to get to the work and at the exact same time, I am trying to appreciate the other kinds of time and other presences and not always wish I were writing. Kind of a paradox.

ST: I am enjoying writing back and forth with you. In a way the further (my) writing strays from the epistolary the less sense it makes to me. This chapbook is concerned very much with how a self arranges itself in the act of confessing, and in the act of hearing, both of which are built in to the epistolary mode. In writing for an unseen audience, however, or in reading the work of an author that is, say, not a friend, not a contemporary, perhaps long dead, this transmission is slightly different. Do you think these various types of communion are discrete entities, or do they exist on some kind of spectrum? Do they partake in the same quality or degree of the imaginal?

JC: Recently Lisa Robertson was reading on my campus. During the Q and A I asked how we keep the writing real and urgent when the pressures of publication (and all that includes) creep up on us. Her response was that we keep our intimates in mind. We write with and for one another (or at least that is how I understood her words). This makes sense to me. I think of Dickinson's poems written on the paper she used to wrap flowers in, or sent in letters. For me writing is almost always grounded in intimacy, and when it's not, it begins to lose energy—I care less about it.

That sense we sometimes have that a writer is speaking our own thoughts, or implanting thoughts directly into our own mind, this sense that as we read we are somehow becoming the author or the book, this deeply invasive/intimate sense of becoming, is what made me a reader/writer. This feels especially powerful when the writer is speaking across a great distance, be that of time, place, or experience. The book is not "relatable" because it tells me what I already know, but is transformative because it makes me someone new. I felt that reading Dickinson when I was a child, I feel it reading Moten now. There's something I don't know I know, or there's a mood, a feeling, an understanding that, as I read, begins to become no longer distinct, no longer estranged, but part of my own envisioning, even as full understanding (whatever that could be) remains always out of reach.

So when we talk about "influence," for me it's not about learning tricks. I could say I was influenced by the blend of prose and poetry in Williams, or by disjunction and play in Hejinian, or by sound in Hopkins. But what really happens, I think, is that reading these writers at some point begins to feel incredibly intimate. I find myself thinking along with them, and feel myself altered as a result.

To return to Lisa Robertson, in an essay on reading titled "Time and the Codex" (from *Nilling*) she writes "Here is the acutely sought ruin of identity. Readings begins in me an elaborate abandonment. Desire and identity are not the same. At times it feels like desire displaces, or replaces identity." Reading, then, and maybe writing, puts one on the edge of an outside of whatever one figures oneself to already be. But that's not to say that we become mechanical, unfeeling, disconnected from our own inner life. Instead writing/reading puts us on that watery, uncertain line between self and other which she calls here "desire." And for this reason I think all writing is epistolary.

Note

1. *The Silence that Fills the Future* is a phrase from Susan Stewart, *Poetry and the Fate of the Senses,* 101.

Printed and bound by CPI Group (UK) Ltd, Croydon, CR0 4YY

09/06/2025

14685644-0001